THE ANGRY SELF

THE ANGRY SELF

A Comprehensive Approach to Anger Management

MIRIAM M. GOTTLIEB, PH.D.

 ZEIG, TUCKER & CO., PUBLISHERS
PHOENIX, ARIZONA

Published by
Zeig, Tucker & Co.
3618 North 24 Street
Phoenix, Arizona 85016

Library of Congress Cataloging-in-Publication Data

Gottlieb, Miriam M., 1949-
    The angry self : a comprehensive approach to anger management /
Miriam M. Gottlieb.
        p.   cm.
    ISBN 1-891944-07-X
    1. Anger.   2. Conflict management.   I. Title.
BF575.A5G67 1998
152.4'7—dc21   98-27880
                                                                    CIP

Manufactured in the United States of America

10 9 8 7 6 5 4 3

▼

NOTE TO COUNSELORS

A number of the forms presented in this book may require duplication, depending on the assignment directions. United States copyright law protects the book; however, the author and publisher grant permission for the duplication of any and all of the following forms for the client's use, as long as they carry the copyright line at the bottom.

Summary Assignment A: Top 10 Frame (p. 17)

Assignment 12: Event Table (p. 33)

Assignment 34: Feelings Frame (p. 96)

Assignment 37: Values Frame (p. 107)

Assignment 40: Crew Member Evaluation Form (p. 113)

Assignment 43: Forced Choices Frame (p. 119)

Assignment 46: Alternatives Frame (p. 125)

Assignment 47: Alternatives Evaluation Frame (p. 128)

Assignment 48: Alternatives Evaluation Frame (p. 130)

Assignment 49: Alternatives Evaluation Frame (p. 132)

▼

C O N T E N T S

▼

A C K N O W L E D G M E N T S

Many people contributed to this project either directly or indirectly. Some of these people were very important to its completion. I would especially like to thank my husband, David, who spent endless hours discussing and challenging ideas for this book, contributing significantly to its humor, and editing it. Thanks to my son, Daniel, who continues to be a constant inspiration and mirror. Thanks also to Jo Ann Krejsta, who patiently reviewed the first attempt and served out huge helpings of encouragement, and to my colleague, Nancy Forrester, who painstakingly corrected every punctuation error and offered valuable ideas. Special thanks to my lifelong friend, Julie Colantonio, who continues to afford moral support and who provided valuable feedback based on her many years of experience as a clinical social worker.

I have always listened carefully to all of my clients. Each has been invaluable in teaching me many important lessons. Most recently, I have also been listening carefully to the graduate students whom I have been lucky enough to supervise in the pursuit of their dreams as future counselors. Their dedication and hope have been an inspiration to me in preparing this workbook. It is hoped that it will make life easier to manage for some people, and will provide counselors with additional tools.

THE ANGRY SELF

▼

INTRODUCTION

As a member of a helping profession—counseling, psychology, social work, the clergy—you have surely had many clients for whom anger was a problem. It may be the presenting symptom, or it may be intertwined with other difficulties. For such a person, either removing the source of the anger or teaching the client to control it is a therapeutic necessity.

This workbook is a tool for you, the professional. At the same time, it is a resource for your client. As you scan through the book, you will see that it is composed of some 46 units. Each of these units contains instructive text for the client (often in the form of a story), and many have exercises designed to help the client learn and retain the skill being taught. The workbook can be given to the client, who reads the text and does the exercises on his or her own, discussing them with you in your sessions. Alternatively, the materials and strategies may be used during sessions, shaped by you to the needs of the individual or group.

This workbook is organized to reflect a therapeutic process that incorporates anger management. It is not meant to be a cookbook on how to deal with the angry client, but is more of a therapeutic journey with a focus on an understanding of the anger problem and of the strategies that have been successful in anger management. The book uses cognitive-behavioral strategies to identify and restructure thinking patterns that precipitate or maintain anger, Ericksonian principles to motivate and expand awareness, and relaxation techniques to address the physical effects of anger. It is drawn from the current research on anger and emotions, as well as from my own research and experience during the 18 years I have been counseling people with anger problems.

I developed this book with a therapeutic sequence in mind, and, therefore, it is most effectively used in this manner. If used as a manual for the selection of strategies only, you need to be cautioned to identify your client's readiness for the strategies.

The book begins with a motivational approach and with rapport building. It uses stories to illustrate the universality of the anger problem and to encourage the client on his or her journey. In recognition of the client's anger problem, it quickly moves into providing the client with strategies to address the immediate problem of anger. Therefore, by following this workbook, the person who is angry learns first to recognize and control his or her anger, and then to use anger's energy to solve the problem that caused the anger.

My clients, especially those who are in much pain, often ask: "How long is this going to take?" This is where your professional judgment is essential. Since this is a therapeutic journey that includes all aspects of a therapeutic process, the length of this journey, as we well know, depends on many factors. To facilitate answering this question, let me describe how this workbook is organized.

There are 46 "units" in the workbook. Each unit will require motivation and active participation, as well as integration of information. The average unit may take about an hour to do. Initially, when the client is in serious need of developing some immediate skills, it may be important to maintain an intense pace. For example, one unit a day is a good pace at which to begin, to allow the individual to learn the skills necessary to start feeling in control. However, as you move along the process, you may find that your client may need to process the information more slowly in order to assure integration of new skills.

If you meet with your client once a week, you may find that the completion of units may also require practice time. Therefore, a good initial pace may be two to three units per week. This will allow you to go over the units with your client, and give you an opportunity to observe his or her ability to learn or to integrate information. You can also give the client further opportunity to practice techniques while creating different scenarios, and help to explain the upcoming units. You will know how much time your specific client will need to become comfortable with the new material as it is presented.

You will begin to see results almost immediately. By the end of the 15th unit (typically, the fifth week), the client will have acquired sufficient skills to be able to control his or her anger in almost all situations. By the midpoint of this workbook, the reader will know how to redirect the energy of anger into a channel where it can be used positively. The workbook concludes by teaching "problem solving," leaving the reader with the ability to evaluate alternatives and to make decisions that really work. Because it is a therapeutic journey, you may find yourself being drawn down different paths. This is fine, but in cases where anger is the true presenting problem, it is initially important to keep the client focused on developing the skills necessary to be safe to himself or herself and others.

Over the years, I have worked with people whose rage threatened to consume them, and with others whose inability to express their anger led to other physical problems. You will meet some of them in this workbook.

If some of the stories and situations in this workbook seem humorous to you, that's fine. If you recognize part of yourself in some of them, that's human. If you think that I am describing a real person and you know who that person is, that's wrong! They are "real"—but as the composites of many individuals. If James and Sharon "come alive" for you or your clients, it is because their experiences, not themselves, are real.

▼

CHAPTER 1

GETTING STARTED

I am going to make anger disappear entirely from your life! Does this sound like a good idea? Do you think we can actually make anger totally disappear? Would you want to? Stop here and take time to think about your answers.

This book will pose many questions. Sometimes they will not have "right" or "wrong" answers, but these first questions do. Why? Anger is an important emotion. Once you learn how to harness its power, it will become your faithful friend. Anger will warn you of potential threats, energize you to meet them, and give you the power to overcome them—but only when you control it.

That's why we don't want to make anger disappear; we want to make it useful. If you opted to make anger disappear, that was probably because it has caused you many difficulties, and you have not yet discovered its positive power. This is what this book is all about—making anger your friend.

Anger Is Like a Wild Horse

Anger is like a wild horse. Try to ride it and you most likely will end up eating dust. Probably you will break something that would better be left whole. Get back on the horse and the "buckin' bronc" will throw you again. You can keep trying, or you can get smart and have someone show you how to tame the animal. Once you have learned to tame a wild horse, you will discover a magical relationship between you and the horse. The animal you tamed will become a good friend.

How is anger like a wild horse? First, if left untamed, anger can be very destructive. Second, most people with an anger problem don't know how to control it and use its power. Third, you can be taught to "tame" your anger, and when you do, it too will become a useful tool and a friend.

In fact, you've already taken the first steps to tame your anger. You recognized that there was something about your life that you wanted to change, and you decided to take action. The next step is this workbook.

▼

In This Corner . . . James

When I think of anger, I am reminded of many people whose anger had serious effects on their lives. See if you recognize any part of yourself in James or Sharon.

James may or may not have had many reasons to be angry, but one thing is sure—James had an anger problem. Outwardly, James was a nice guy; he was friendly, had good manners, and exhibited a sharp wit—most of the time. However, when he became angry, he was like a runaway car, demolishing everything in his path. People who knew him were confused. How could such an apparently caring young man hurt others in such an uncaring way? And hurt others he did, because James had not yet discovered the power of his anger, or the brakes for his runaway car.

One day, James became angry at another young man, Steven. Even James doesn't know what started it or why his anger so quickly grew beyond control. He does remember picking up a baseball bat, and launching a blow aimed directly at Steven's head. Looking back, James felt he was very lucky. His victim had managed to bring up an arm to protect his head, so the blow shattered Steven's arm instead of possibly killing him.

James vividly remembers the boy's twisted arm and his pitiful screams. He had never gone this far before, and he had never been aware of another's pain until that moment. You might say that James had received a wake-up call. But was it too late?

After taking their son to a hospital, Steven's parents called the police and pressed charges against James. James was in serious trouble. He was arrested, and there was talk about charging him with attempted murder, but in the end, James pleaded guilty to assault with a deadly weapon. Since his previous experiences with the law had been relatively minor, James got a break. Instead of going to prison, he was sent to a juvenile corrections institution, where I was working as a psychologist at the time. Many of the young people there would not readily accept help from a psychologist. Many thought that psychologists were for crazy people. But James was different. He was a truly caring young man who did not want to hurt another human being ever again. He was anxious to be helped. And thus began our journey together.

You will meet James many times in this book. Often I will tell you how he responded to the same questions you will be answering.

And in the Other Corner . . . Sharon

Sharon was not in trouble with the law when I met her. In fact, she and I were fellow graduate students. Sharon was studious, mild-mannered, smart, and very considerate. You wouldn't guess that she had lived in an emotionally abusive relationship for many years. One day she told me that she was seeing a therapist. When I asked why, she told me her story.

"It started out just like any other day," she began in a barely audible voice. "I came home from work, did a little cleaning, and started to cook dinner. Clark, my husband, came home from work, tossed his dirty jacket on the nearest chair, and made straight for the dinner table. I don't think he said a single word to me except to demand his supper.

"So, I dropped what I was doing and rushed dinner to the table. We were having spaghetti with tomato sauce—his favorite. We started to eat and I made some small talk and he did his usual thing: complain. He criticized my hair, the appearance of the house, the food (while greedily shoveling in mouthful after mouthful), and anything else he could think of.

"I realized I was starting to get annoyed. It was not that his complaints and demands were anything new. Maybe I just had had enough. I looked at him, talking with his mouth full, with sauce dripping from the sides of his mouth, and the horror of it all suddenly struck me. I guess I just lost it."

At this point, it was interesting to notice a subtle transformation in Sharon. She no longer appeared to be the quiet, mild-mannered student. She stood tall; her shoulders were squared. A small smile appeared on her face and she wore a gentle look of surprise. As she continued with the story, I realized that she was reliving the feelings she had experienced that night.

"I picked up my plate of spaghetti," she went on, "just loaded with tomato sauce, and I threw it at him. The plate didn't actually hit him—but the food did. You should have seen the look on his face. Well, you couldn't really see much of his face, but I could tell he was just about as surprised as I was."

I asked her how she felt after throwing the dinner plate, and Sharon began describing a whole set of emotions. "At first, I was mostly surprised, but pretty soon I just felt dismayed. This was not me— I don't usually go around throwing things at people. But this time, it made me feel strong. And that scared me a little."

Sharon went on to say that for years she had been burdened by an unspoken smoldering anger. She had never shown it (we call this "stuffing" anger), and when she finally recognized this anger and expressed it, she experienced a strong sense of liberation. However, she was fully aware of what could have happened if the plate had struck her husband. She said she was horrified—she did not want to become like him.

Sharon needed to learn to express anger instead of holding it in until it built up beyond control. How do you think she accomplished this? What happened to Clark? Did they get the stains out of the carpet? Will Clark ever eat spaghetti with tomato sauce again?

A Time and Place for Anger

Everything has its time and place, and anger is no exception.

In 1965, the United States began a secret military mission in Vietnam. By 1969, this "mission" had grown into a full-scale war. For young men living through those times, it was bad enough having to face going into the army and possibly being killed, but it was far worse for those who believed the war to be unjust and unnecessary.

Many young people became very angry. I saw their faces: angry faces of people I knew, and hundreds of other angry faces of people I would meet. For a few, this anger brought out destructive impulses, but for most of them, it was energizing and focused on trying to protest injustice.

One very hot summer's day, over 500,000 people gathered in Washington, D.C., overflowing the grounds of the Washington Monument and covering every open space within a mile. Anger had brought them there. They listened to speeches, but mostly they were just present, supporting each other and sending a powerful message that the rest of the country could not fail to hear.

There was virtually no violence. The anger of half a million people found expression in little more than being together. United by the common goal of preserving aspects of humanity that were in danger of being lost, they made their anger work for them in the only way that could have achieved its purpose. And it did; many believe that their protest march was the beginning of the end of the Vietnam war.

> **SUMMARY:** Anger doesn't always have to start a war— sometimes it can end one.

Look at All the Angry People . . .

And so I remember the many faces of anger; James, who was incarcerated; Sharon, who stuffed her anger; and the young men and young women protesting a war, searching for justice and peace.

Angry faces can be frightening, because anger can be a very powerful emotion. But anger is also a normal, healthy emotion. It becomes a problem when it is expressed in a way that hurts you or others, or when it is the only feeling you allow yourself to experience. If anger is not channeled or expressed in a healthy manner, it can lead to destructive behaviors. Here are some of them.

▸ Holding anger in until it explodes
▸ Trashing your room
▸ Punching walls or throwing things around
▸ Abusing others (anywhere from name calling to hitting)
▸ Using alcohol or drugs to calm down
▸ Neglecting responsibilities
▸ Running away
▸ Experiencing physical aches and pains related to stress
▸ Destroying property

Do any of these behaviors sound a bit like you when you are angry? Do you hurt yourself or other people? Has anger affected your social relationships? Are you unpleasant to be around because you might "go off" at any time? If you answered "yes" (or even "maybe") to any of these questions, this workbook is for you.

Where This Journey Will Take You—and How This Book Works

If you wanted to increase your strength, you might go to a gym. Someone would show you how to use the equipment and how to do the exercises. But if you did each one a couple of times and then went home, it wouldn't do much good.

This book works in the same way. As you learn things, your counselor will ask you to complete assignments from the workbook. Some may seem pointless to you. Some may be difficult. But they are all part of the process of learning a new and powerful skill. So participate actively in the assignments as they come up.

If you don't completely understand an assignment, read the chapter again or discuss it with your counselor. Do your best, but never hesitate to ask for help. Attempting a hard assignment is like trying to do a hard exercise; it generally does more good than an easy one does. Stretch your mind just as you would stretch your muscles. After you finish a set of push-ups, you don't expect your arms to bulk up suddenly, and neither will these assignments provide you instantly with amazing new skills. But, day by day, you will see results and you will get stronger.

So What's the Program?

This workbook has eight more chapters. Each deals with an important group of skills, and each builds on the chapters before it. The chapters are divided into "units" that are short enough so that you can usually finish one without interruption. Work with your counselor to establish a schedule that is comfortable for you. Don't try to do too many at once—give yourself time to understand what you have learned before moving on to the next unit. Give your muscles a chance to rebuild.

Now it's time for your first assignment.

ASSIGNMENT 1

Directions:

1. Get a notebook. You are going to use this as your "anger journal." You can decorate it anyway you want. Each time you get angry, take out your journal and describe what happened. Here's what to include:

- The time and where you were when you became angry
- What made you angry—what you were feeling and thinking
- What you did when you became angry
- The consequences of your angry behavior

After you have reached the part of this workbook where you learn coping strategies, you will also start to include:

- The coping strategies or alternatives you could or did use
- Your reason for choosing the strategy you did

2. You will also need another notebook to use in doing exercises. You can use a separate notebook or set aside space in the back of your anger journal.

▼

CHAPTER 2

RECOGNIZING ANGER

You might say, "It's easy to tell when I'm angry—I hit somebody." Very good; you have successfully recognized your anger. But you recognized it a little too late. In this chapter, you will learn to identify the way you look and feel *before* you get uncontrollably angry. This is a necessary first step, since there is very little I can teach you to do when there already is blood on the ground.

◄◄ **UNIT 1** ►►

INTRODUCING THE "ANGER RULER"

James Almost Meets His Caseworker

For James, it was his first day in the juvenile correctional institution. He was in a small interview room where he would meet his caseworker—the man assigned to watch over him and to coordinate the services he would receive.

James walked over to the tiny window and looked out, a frown on his face. If you saw him from a distance, you might have guessed that he was deep in thought. If so, you would have guessed wrong. But things often look different from a distance. As you got closer to James, you would begin to see a certain tension and a sharp kind of energy. The caseworker, Jason Shields, saw them and decided to leave James alone.

Mr. Shields could sense that James was angry. If he had asked him how he felt, James probably would not have answered. This was James' way when he was angry at himself. His caseworker had seen these signs many times before. So he left the room, waiting for a time when James would feel less angry.

The Anger Ruler

It is not always easy to recognize when other people are angry. Mr. Shields could tell, because he had seen many angry faces at this institution throughout the years. But most of us don't have this range of experience; sometimes it is even hard to recognize our own anger.

Anger has many different faces, and it comes in different colors, shapes, and sizes. Remember the Incredible Hulk? As a symbol of anger, he was big, green, and ugly! You probably are aware when you are in the "Incredible Hulk" stage of anger, but what about the other times when you are just annoyed, or when your anger is only beginning to build up? Can you recognize these stages of anger?

Let's illustrate the levels of anger by using a rating scale, or "Anger Ruler."

ANGER RULER

mildly angry				ANGRY				SUPER ANGRY	
1	2	3	4	5	6	7	8	9	10

Would you recognize anger when it is at the number 1 or 3 stage? Perhaps you wouldn't even call it anger. Let's attach some other types of labels to the Anger Ruler.

ASSIGNMENT 2

Directions:

1. On a piece of paper, draw an Anger Ruler like the one above. Underneath the 1 or 2, write the name of a color that you associate with mild anger. Under 5 or 6, write a color that means moderate anger to you. Under 9 or 10, write a color you think of when you think of strong anger.

2. Write each of the following words or phrases underneath the Anger Ruler where you feel it fits:

> smooth ball
> rough rock
> jagged piece of glass
> tiny
> man-sized
> huge
> irritated
> upset
> ferocious

3. Think of a few other words or phrases that you can place under the Anger Ruler.

▼

COMMENTS ON ASSIGNMENT 2

Take a look at your work. You have accomplished something important. You have noticed the difference between different degrees of anger. From here, it's not such a big step to recognizing these levels in your own feelings and actions. That is what we are going to do next.

◀◀ **UNIT 2** ▶▶

THE TYPES OF ANGER SIGNS

Behavioral Signs

The first step in learning to recognize levels of anger is to become aware of anger cues or anger signs. When someone says, "You're really gonna get it now" during an argument, this is an obvious verbal sign that the person is angry. If that same person makes a fist and starts striding purposefully toward you, this is a further sign of anger. We call these "behavioral" signs because we see them in people's behavior. It is important to recognize these signs in another person, so that you can wisely withdraw (in other words, "run") if you are not ready for a fight. It is just as important to see these signs in yourself.

Physical Signs

Signs are very important. When you drive a car, you learn to depend on signs, such as stop signs, pedestrian crossing signs, and traffic lights. These are the highway's physical signs. They can be very useful. For example, correctly reading a traffic light is essential to driving safely. It provides information that allows you to make decisions about your own and other people's safety. Pedestrian crossing signs warn us that people may be walking across the road. Since society frowns on running down little old ladies at a crosswalk, you should respond to this sign by exercising a bit of caution—unless you want to share a room with James for a while.

Your body gives you a lot of physical signs when you get angry. For example, when you first start getting angry, you might begin to sweat or feel hot. Of course, you might also sweat and feel hot when you play basketball. When you are angry, however, it is a "different kind" of hot and sweaty. And you will know it as you start to learn the physical signs your body gives you at different stages of anger.

A World Without Signs

Imagine you are driving on a highway. It's a beautiful day and there's no one on the road but you. You start to feel good and your foot presses down on the accelerator. There are no road signs—no speed limit signs, no curve warnings, no exit signs. The pavement is smooth and dry and your car is behaving beautifully. Gradually you increase your speed—60, 70, 80 miles per hour.

The broad highway stretches before you for miles. The road is all yours. There is no one to tell you what to do or to place limits on you. You're not worried by the lack of road signs. At 110, you decide to find out how fast your car will go as soon as you get past this short uphill stretch.

You reach the top of a hill. Finally, you see a sign. It says: "Construction—Pavement Ends 200 Feet." At 115 miles per hour, you've got about one second to stop your car. That's not enough time. About all you do have time for is a fleeting thought: "Why wasn't there a warning sign much earlier?" If you're having a lucky day, at the other side of the construction sign will be smooth, hard dirt, and you might have a chance to stop. Otherwise . . .

For James, anger felt just this way. He didn't recognize when his anger was picking up speed. There were signs—physical and behavioral—but James didn't see them. By the time James knew he was angry, he was already going at full speed, and didn't have the braking power to stop. The best he could hope for was a smooth hard road (such as a friend breaking up the fight), but sometimes he wasn't so lucky.

Reading the Signs

You must learn to recognize your signs and to read them correctly. Some signs are very easy to read. The flashing lights and swinging gates at a railroad crossing are hard to miss. Other signs are more subtle. Gauges and dials on a car's dashboard present a lot of valuable information, such as the engine's temperature. But you have to learn how to read them and to understand what they look like when your car has a problem.

Engineers have added "idiot" lights to cars, such as one that says, "Engine Hot," to help people who haven't learned to read the gauges. I have good news for you, and I have bad news. The bad news is that your body doesn't have "idiot" lights. The good news it that you won't need them after you finish this chapter.

The Anger Ruler we used in the previous unit is exactly like a car's temperature gauge. It will prove very useful throughout this book. Please take time to do Assignment 3 while you start to think about what physical and behavioral signs your body sends to you.

ASSIGNMENT 3

Directions:

1. Make a permanent Anger Ruler, one that you can carry with you in your folder. You can use a piece of cardboard and, if possible, have it laminated so that it will last. Place the numbers 1 through 10 on it as on the Anger Ruler in Unit 1. You don't have to write the words "mildly angry," "ANGRY," and "SUPER ANGRY" on it, unless you want to.

Feel free to color or decorate your Anger Ruler in any way that feels right to you.

While you are making your ruler, see if you can come up with one word or phrase for each of the 10 numbers. You can use types of weather ("1" might be "breeze" and "10" "tornado"), or bodies of water ("1" = creek, "10" = raging torrent), or any other symbols that work for you.

◀◀ UNIT 3 ▶▶
PHYSICAL SIGNS OF ANGER

Another Tool: The Physical Signs Frame

In this unit, you will meet and use the first of this workbook's "frames"—the Physical Signs Frame. A frame is just a form that you can fill out, and there will be many others as you proceed. The frames are bound into the workbook so that you can find them easily if you need to go back to them later.

A physical sign is what your body does and how it feels. Various emotions trigger physical signs. For example, when you are amused, your mouth curves upward in a smile, and you may even laugh.

Anger has its own set of physical signs. Your signs may be different from mine, but almost everybody exhibits some of them. Can you think of a physical sign of anger? A common one is a tightening of the muscles.

These physical signs can be your warning lights; they can tell you to stop and check things out. We are going to identify your warning signs by recording how your body feels when you are calm and how it feels when you are angry.

Start by sitting down. Close your eyes for a moment and really think about your body. Focus on how your body fits into and feels in the chair. Shift your position a little. Which muscles did you move? Was there a tiny bit of discomfort? Did you move your bottom a bit to "settle in"?

Keep focusing on your physical sensations while you cross your legs. This awareness may be a bit uncomfortable at first because you may be noticing the little twinges and pains that you usually ignore. It may be hard to get into a really good position because almost every position has its own discomforts. This may not be a good way to live your life, but it's a great way to discover your physical signs.

Here is where the Physical Signs Frame comes in. We are going to record how each part of your body feels by writing the sensations you experience in one of these frames. To give you an idea of how to fill one out, I did this one just after my favorite basketball team, the Phoenix Suns, blew a big lead and lost an important game. For those items where I didn't feel any body sensations, I wrote "None."

▼

WHAT YOU WERE DOING	
Just finished watching Suns blow a 16-point lead to Portland.	
ITEM	**HOW YOUR BODY FELT**
Body position	Sitting in the kitchen, slumped over the table.
Arms	Folded in front—head resting on them.
Hands	Tightly clenched.
Legs	Tense.
Feet	Muscles tensed and slightly sore from being pressed hard against the floor.
Neck and shoulders	Shoulders tight; slight pain across the top of my back (neck strain?).
Jaw	Tense; teeth clenched together.
Mouth	None.
Eyes	Closed.
Other	None.

When you think you understand what the Physical Signs Frame is all about, do Assignment 4.

ASSIGNMENT 4

Directions:

1. Sitting in your chair, try to make yourself as calm as possible. Just relax. Think pleasant thoughts for a minute or so, and then fill out the following Physical Signs Frame. If you feel relaxed, light, or limp, write these reactions down.

▼

WHAT YOU WERE DOING	
Sitting calmly.	
ITEM	**HOW YOUR BODY FELT**
Body position	
Arms	
Hands	
Legs	
Feet	
Neck and shoulders	
Jaw	
Mouth	
Eyes	
Other	

COMMENTS ON ASSIGNMENT 4

If you have written "None" in most of the boxes, put this assignment away and take a break. Come back to it later and try to concentrate on it. Your counselor can help if you are still having trouble.

You Get to Be an Actor

When you have become sufficiently aware of your body and how it feels when you are calmly sitting down, take a moment to remember the last time you were angry. Try to remember why you were angry. You may actually start feeling angry again—this is fine. If you do not start feeling angry while you are remembering, become an actor. Remember your previous anger and make your body look and feel as it did then. Take your time. *Keep your focus on your body, not on the anger itself.* Now fill out another Physical Signs Frame.

▼

ASSIGNMENT 5

Directions:

1. Fill out a Physical Signs Frame for what your body feels like when it is angry.

WHAT YOU WERE DOING	
Feeling angry.	
ITEM	**HOW YOUR BODY FELT**
Body position	
Arms	
Hands	
Legs	
Feet	
Neck and shoulders	
Jaw	
Mouth	
Eyes	
Other	

◀◀ **UNIT 4** ▶▶

RECOGNIZING PHYSICAL SIGNS IN OTHERS

If This Seems to Be Going a Little Slowly . . .

Many of the skills you will be shown in this workbook are easy to learn. All you will need to do is read about them, try them once or twice, and then go on. But recognizing anger signs takes practice. It may begin to seem as though you are not making progress fast enough, but you are! Once you finish this chapter, you will be past the steepest part of that mountain you are trying to climb.

Let's see where we are so far. You have thought about and written down how your body feels when you are angry and when you are not angry. The signs we have been looking for so far are those that are easily recognized in ourselves. But there are other signs that are more easily seen in other people. For example, some common signs of anger are sweating, a red face, fast breathing, enlarged nostrils, and a heaving chest. These are easy to note in others, but we tend to ignore them when describing our own physical feelings.

Getting a Bit of Help

Many times in this workbook you will be given assignments that require a "helper." Your counselor may be your helper, or you may be told to use a family member, a friend, or a teacher. You can also do these assignments alone, but it is more fun to do them with someone else, and you get more out of it this way. Talk this over with your counselor and decide who your helpers will be.

Things to Look for

In Assignments 6 and 7, you are going to be looking for physical signs of anger in other people. What signs should you look for? You can start with the sort of physical signs you observed in yourself in Assignment 5. You might also look for the ones we talked about earlier in this unit. You will probably find a few others that we have not thought of so far. Anything the body does is a physical sign.

ASSIGNMENT 6

Directions:

1. In this assignment, you are going to remember physical signs of anger in people you know. Pick one or two people whom you have seen angry. If you are working with a helper, he or she should also choose one or two people. If you both know the same angry people—that's even better.

Think back carefully to how each of these people looked when he or she was angry. Close your eyes if it helps you to visualize. Take your time and try to "see" the angry person in your mind, studying his or her posture, movements, color, breathing, and other details of appearance.

Record the anger signs you recall on a piece of paper.

2. When you are finished recording your observations, share them with your helper. If you both used the same person, how closely do your signs agree? Were any of the anger signs you observed in others the same as those you recorded about yourself in Assignment 5?

Evaluating the Actors

We are going to do one more exercise in recognizing physical anger signs. This time, we are going to observe actors pretending they are angry. If the actors are doing their jobs well, we should be able to see their anger signs clearly.

Once again, this assignment is best done with a helper.

ASSIGNMENT 7

Directions:

1. Choose a television show in which there are likely to be angry scenes. Almost any dramatic show will do; even soap operas sometimes furnish scenes of dramatic anger. Watch the show with your helper. When an angry scene begins, pick a character to observe. You and your helper

should observe the same character. Then turn off the sound. You are going to look for physical signs of anger, so the dialog would only get in the way.

Record the physical signs of anger you observed on a sheet of paper.

2. Compare your results with those of your helper. How similar are they? Did you see some of the signs you previously noted in Assignments 5 and 6 again? Were there any new signs?

3. Do this exercise again with a different scene and a different character. You should repeat steps 1 and 2 for at least two or three scenes.

4. When you are finished, think about all of the anger signs you have seen in others. Were there any signs you saw in them that you think also apply to yourself, but which you did not write down in Assignment 5? If there were, take out Assignment 5 and add the new signs to it.

5. Did the actors do a good job of showing anger? Could they have done better? How? Don't be too hard on them—you yourself are going to have a chance to act in the next unit!

◄◄ UNIT 5 ►►
SEEING PHYSICAL SIGNS IN YOURSELF

Use All of Your Senses

Up to this point, you have been identifying all of the physical signs of anger you could find. In this unit, you are going to finish this process by becoming an actor. For this, you are going to need three things: your Anger Ruler, the Physical Signs Frame from Assignment 5, and a large mirror, preferably one in which you can see your entire body.

We will start with a simple exercise. Look into the mirror and make an angry face. Examine your face in detail—look at all of the muscles that are working hard. Now use another of your senses. Touch each muscle group: the frown, the clenched jaw, the squinting eyes, the compressed lips. Try to remember how these muscles feel. Notice whether or not you have a particular taste sensation. Perhaps you are breathing rapidly; in that case, your sense of smell may behave differently from usual.

Do this exercise a few times. You are looking for some new physical signs to add to Assignment 5. For some people, these nonvisual signs (touch, hearing, smell, taste) are strong indications of anger. While you are doing this exercise, take out your Anger Ruler and judge yourself. How angry a face did you make? Could you get anywhere near 10 on the Anger Ruler?

Starting Your Acting Career

Now we are going to put everything together. You know your physical anger signs. In Assignment 8, use them to act out an angry scene in front of the mirror. Think about something that made you angry in the past, or invent something new that would definitely make you angry. Before you start, here are a few ground rules.

► We do not want to disturb the neighbors or summon the police, so no shouting. In fact, no speaking at all. You can mouth words and pretend to shout, but don't saying anything out loud. We want to focus on your physical signs, not on the extent of your cussing vocabulary.

▶ In the course of your acting, you may make threatening moves or gestures. This is okay, but stop short of hitting anything. By the time you have resorted to violence, the exercise is over. We are looking for anger signs to use to prevent violence.

▶ Use your own anger signs. Don't use signs that you saw in other people but do not normally use yourself.

This is an important assignment. You may want to repeat it several times. You can also have your helper watch and give you feedback. Your helper may even want to try anger acting;—then you can give him or her feedback and become a critic too!

Assignment 8 uses your Anger Ruler. If you do not want to mark it up, get an "anger marker" that you can place on the scale—a paper clip, a piece of paper with an arrow drawn on it, or anything else handy.

ASSIGNMENT 8

Directions:

1. Review your Physical Signs Frame from Assignment 5. These are your anger signs.

2. Pick a past event that made you angry, or make up something that definitely would make you angry. Think about it and "see" the event clearly in your mind.

3. Step in front of the mirror and act out the event. While you are doing this, notice your physical signs of anger and remember them. You might want to try acting the scene several times until you "get it right."

4. On a piece of paper, write down the physical signs of anger you noticed.

5. On the Anger Ruler, place a marker on the anger level you just displayed.

6. How good an acting job did you do?

7. Update your Physical Signs Frame if you discovered any new signs.

Repetitions:

Repeat this assignment with at least two different anger scenes. You can do more if you enjoy it. This exercise is very helpful in building up your ability to see your own signs of anger.

SUMMARY ASSIGNMENT A

Directions:

Summarize what you have learned about your physical signs of anger by filling in the following Top 10 Frame (extra blank frames are available from your counselor). On line 1, write the anger sign that occurs most frequently and strongly for you. Continue with the other anger signs you observed in order of their strength.

▼

TOP 10 LIST OF . . .	
Physical anger signs	
NUMBER	**ITEM**
1	
2	
3	
4	
5	
6	
7	
8	
9	
10	

Reproduced from *The Angry Self: A Comprehensive Approach to Anger Management,* © 1999, Zeig, Tucker & Co., Publishers.

◀◀ UNIT 6 ▶▶
SIGNS OF ANGER/SIGNS OF FEAR

This unit is partly for practice and partly for fun. There are no formal assignments, but you should do the exercises anyway. We also will get our first glimpse of how anger can be an important and useful tool.

Your Limited Set of Physical Reactions

I have had two ferrets as pets, Squeaky and Slinky. They were very different from each other. Squeaky was the inquisitive ferret, and Slinky was the athletic one (ferrets are members of the weasel family). One day, I noticed Slinky scratching himself vigorously around his neck. When he kept on scratching for days, I took him to the veterinarian. She told me that he probably just had a stomach ache. "Well," I said, "if he has a stomach ache, why is he scratching his *neck*?" The answer was surprising to me.

The veterinarian said that this ferret had only learned a small number of physical responses. He had learned that when he had an itch, scratching his neck helped. When he had a stomach pain, he tried all of the physical responses he knew, and for some reason settled on neck scratching as the "best of a bad lot." This was his attempt at getting relief.

You are, of course, much smarter than the ferret, and you have a much greater number of physical responses. Still, your body's physical reactions to emotions are limited. Therefore, your body may react in much the same way to two different emotions. Emotions that often bring out similar physical reactions are anger, fear, and surprise. We are going to see how these are related, and in so doing, we will begin to understand why you need anger.

Two-Year-Olds Tell Us a Lot About Ourselves

First, let's look at these emotions in a very young child (about two or three years old). Let's call him Jimmy.

It is easy to tell when Jimmy is very angry. He clenches his fist, every muscle in his body seems to tighten up, his face gets red, and he even bares his teeth a little. These are his physical signs of anger. If you filled out a Physical Signs Frame for Jimmy, it would probably contain a lot of the same signs you saw in yourself. However, for Jimmy, his physical anger signs are usually followed by a tantrum. He will either stomp his feet and wave his arms furiously, or try to hit anyone around him, all the while wailing desperately. This is probably before he throws himself on the floor and does his dying-roach imitation. (Jimmy's stomping and loud crying are behavioral signs, not physical signs; we'll talk about these in the next unit.)

One day, Jimmy was outside with his mother. A strange dog down the street started barking loudly. Jimmy got scared. Many of his physical signs were the same as those he used when he was angry (his face was red and his fists were clenched). But his behaviors were very different. The first thing Jimmy did was run to his mother for safety and clutch at her dress.

The message the brain receives and the chemical response the brain makes are very similar for both anger and fear. Our first, most primitive responses to both emotions are almost identical. If Jimmy's mother fails to comfort the child quickly, his fear may reach desperate proportions and he may begin to behave just as he did when he was angry. (There are also important physical differences between anger and fear, but a detailed biological discussion lies outside of the scope of this workbook.)

Your Response to Fear and Surprise

Jimmy's reactions can teach us a great deal, but before we draw any conclusions, let's check out your own physical reactions to different emotions. You have already recorded your physical signs of anger. Now try the same thing with fear.

Go back to the mirror. Imagine an event that made, or could make, you very fearful. Then act out that event in front of the mirror and make a note of your physical responses. Compare them with your anger signs. Probably there are some that are the same, but others that differ.

Surprise is another emotion that has similarities to anger and fear. Do the mirror acting bit again, this time using an event that greatly surprised you.

Now review the physical signs of these three emotions. How are they similar? How are they different?

Distinguishing Among Fear, Anger, and Surprise

This section is fairly advanced. After reading it, you will probably have additional questions; you might not understand it completely. A good idea is to jot down your questions and discuss them with your counselor when you get a chance.

Although the physical signs of fear, anger, and surprise are similar, they are not identical emotions. The experts are far from agreement on this subject, but I am now going to try to explain the similarities and differences among fear, surprise, and anger.

Of the three, fear is the easiest to define. Fear is a "primitive" reaction to a threat to your survival. Most animals more complex than a jellyfish experience fear. Their reaction is almost always one of three alternatives: fight, flight, or freeze. In animals, the decision as whether to fight, run away, or do nothing is based on such considerations as size, posture, or other aspects of physical appearance. In many ways, humans behave like animals. We also experience fear, and an instinctive part of our brain responds with an urge to fight or flee. Sometimes people become "paralyzed with fear," unable to do anything. This may occur in cases where neither the flight nor fight option is acceptable.

Surprise is much like fear, except that the event that caused the surprise is only *potentially* a threat. We need more information before we can tell whether or not we are under attack. For example, if another person screams unexpectedly, you will be startled. Your surprise reaction occurs because the scream might signify a threat to you, but you are not sure. You can't decide whether fight or flight is warranted until you know more about what caused the scream.

For both fear and surprise, the threat (or possible threat) is to your *physical* survival or health. Anger is different—anger is a response to a threat to your *emotional* health.

Here is an example. You are walking down the street with friends when a man confronts you. He starts yelling and accusing you of being a coward. You begin to get *angry*, because this is a threat to your emotional health, specifically to your self-esteem. You are not a coward and you resent hearing this stranger call you one. Now he suddenly puts his hand under his coat; you are *surprised*. Could this be a threat? When he pulls out a gun, you know. You experience *fear* because your physical survival is threatened. In a few moments (if he doesn't pull the trigger, of course), you begin to experience additional *anger*. Again, it has become a threat to your self-esteem — what will your friends think if you back down? Later in this workbook, you will learn how to keep both your self-esteem and your life.

This example shows how fear and anger differ, but it also shows that they often are virtually inseparable. In the above situation, could you quickly tell where fear ended and anger began? I could not. Fortunately, I don't have to. We are going to learn (in Chapter 3) that our first task in response to fear and anger should be the same. That task is to identify the threat. Then we can select the course of action that most benefits us.

So, it would not be correct to say that every time you experience one of your anger signs you must be angry. It might be the sign of another emotion. But you know enough about yourself now to distinguish the signs of anger from those of other emotions, although it may take you a few seconds to figure it out.

These few seconds can be very valuable to you. Suppose, for example, you are camping in the woods and a bear breaks into your tent and steals the food you were going to eat for dinner. Your first reaction is fear (after all, it *is* a very big bear). What you do now could be extremely important.

If you recognize your feeling for what it is, fear, you can do the logical thing—run. You won't get your food back, but you won't become bear food either.

If you don't recognize your reactions correctly, your fear may become anger. If your anger gets the best of you, you might do something foolish, such as chasing the bear to recover your food.

It is important to distinguish among fear, surprise, and anger (and other emotions) so that you can make your best response to each. You now have the skills to do just that. After finishing this chapter, which ends with a discussion of behavioral signs, you are going to learn exactly what you can accomplish because of these skills.

James Fails to Distinguish Between Emotions

During one therapy session, James told me about a fight he had when he was 15. He and some friends were playing basketball when James was fouled by another player. The penalty for the foul was two free throws, so James stepped up to the free-throw line, bounced the basketball once, took aim— and missed the shot by six feet. The reason he missed was that his girlfriend thought it would be funny to sneak up behind him and poke him in the side just as he took his shot.

James' emotion was surprise. Unfortunately, he failed to recognize it, so that by the time he had turned around to find out what happened, it had already turned to anger. He shouted at his girlfriend, who felt hurt and began to cry. James realized his mistake and tried to apologize. The whole scene was something everyone would like to forget. The most successful "forgetter" was James' girlfriend—she forgot that she had ever liked James. James lost a lot of friends that way.

> **SUMMARY:** You now have the skills to distinguish among fear, anger, and surprise. From now on, when you experience one of your physical signs, immediately ask yourself whether it's "fear, anger, or surprise." Simply identifying your emotion will save you from scenes such as the one James went through.

Adrenaline and Other Brain Chemicals

You have seen how fear and surprise may result in physical signs very similar to those of anger. This is not surprising, since our body helps us protect ourselves by releasing adrenaline when we might think we are in danger. This adrenaline, plus other chemical changes in the brain, causes many of the physical signs. How we deal with this surge of adrenaline in our body is another story, one we will talk about later.

Adrenaline is not evil, however. In fact, it is a crucial survival factor for humans and similar animals. It gives you extra strength and speed during an emergency. Sometimes the emotion of anger indicates that such an emergency exists.

Imagine that you are home alone one night. Suddenly you hear the sound of a window breaking. You investigate and see a man entering your home. He has a gun. Your first emotion is fear, and you react by trying to escape. But you can't; the only exits are locked or would force you into the intruder's field of fire. You hear him smashing your television set. Fear slowly gives way to anger. As the sounds indicate that the intruder is trashing your home, your anger grows. The adrenaline starts to flow. Now you hear his steps approaching the place where you are hiding and you know you will be discovered in a few moments. You grab a broom, jump out of your hiding place, and jab the gunman in the gut as hard as you can. Your blow has extra strength because of the adrenaline, and you run faster, getting through the back door before the intruder can recover. Anger, and your body's reaction to it, may have saved your life. That is why nature gave it to you. But only because you recognized fear and then recognized anger could you use them both effectively.

◄◄ UNIT 7 ►►
BEHAVIORAL SIGNS OF ANGER

Our goal in this chapter has been to learn to recognize our anger. To do this, you learned your own physical signs. This is an excellent way to tell when you are angry, but sometimes the physical signs are subtle or we just don't notice them. In this case, there is another set of signs of anger for us to read. These are called behavioral signs.

Sharon Learns More About Herself

Behavioral signs are things that you do when you are angry. For example, Sharon threw a plate of food and James hit people with handy objects. We all have these behaviors, but mine and yours might be very different. After the class at which Sharon told her "spaghetti" story, we all went to a coffee house. I happened to sit next to Sharon, and I asked her if she had ever become angry at her husband before the plate-throwing incident.

At first, she said she never had, but then she thought about it. Sharon had gone to a psychologist after the spaghetti-throwing incident, both to try to save her marriage and to try to understand herself better. One of the first things she learned was to stop denying how she felt. Now she was thinking hard about her past and not allowing herself to cover up her feelings.

"I guess I really did get angry at him a lot of times," she said, "but I never showed it." Just then, the waitress came to serve our coffee and desserts. One of the people in our group gave her a hard time, insisting that he had ordered one dessert when actually he had ordered another. The waitress apologized and said she would be right back with the other dessert. As she left the table, we heard her humming to herself.

Sharon stared after her as if remembering something long past. "I used to do that," she began. "When Clark said something mean, I would just turn away from him, and, if I was really annoyed, I would hum something. I remember one time when he said that his soup was cold and ordered me to heat it up. I must have started to hum something he didn't like, because he just exploded. He wanted to know why I always went around humming some 'stupid' song. Of course, I stopped humming, but then I started to get so upset that I actually turned around and stomped my foot. When he looked up, I pretended I tripped, but if he had pushed me just a little bit more, he might have ended up with soup in his lap instead of spaghetti on his face."

She laughed a little, and then concluded: "I wonder which he would have liked better." It was supposed to be a joke and we all laughed politely. Actually, Sharon, who said she never showed her anger, revealed three behavioral signs in her story, not counting her favorite one of throwing food. Can you identify them? Read the preceding paragraph again if you have to.

Sharon's behavioral signs were:
▶ Turning away
▶ Humming
▶ Stomping her foot
▶ Throwing food

Like most people, Sharon exhibited these signs at different levels of anger. On your Anger Ruler, mark the level of anger for each of these signs.

Your Behavioral Signs

Behavioral signs tend to be very consistent in terms of the anger levels they show. Sharon hummed when she was more than a little annoyed, but long before she lost any of her rigid control. She would never have stomped her foot when she was only "turning away angry." It's probably the same way with you. This next assignment will help you identify your behavioral signs.

ASSIGNMENT 9

Directions:

1. Think about a recent time when you became angry. Picture the event in your mind, starting at the beginning. Identify the things you did—your behaviors—at each stage of your anger. Use the following Behavioral Signs Frame to record your results. To help you understand this tool, I have filled out the first one for Sharon's humming episode.

2. Repeat this exercise with another time you got angry.

3. Using a third Behavioral Signs Frame, list as many of your other angry behaviors as you can remember. Report both what you do when you are really angry and what you do when you are only mildly angry.

EVENT YOU ARE DESCRIBING	
(for Sharon) Foot-stomping when Clark complained about cold soup and my humming.	
ANGER LEVEL	**BEHAVIOR**
1	
2	Turning my back.
3	
4	Humming.
5	
6	
7	Stomping my foot.
8	
9	Dumping soup in his lap (I did not get this far).
10	

▼

BEHAVIORAL SIGNS FRAME

EVENT YOU ARE DESCRIBING	
My angry event #1:	

ANGER LEVEL	BEHAVIOR
1	
2	
3	
4	
5	
6	
7	
8	
9	
10	

▼

BEHAVIORAL SIGNS FRAME

EVENT YOU ARE DESCRIBING	
My angry event #2:	

ANGER LEVEL	BEHAVIOR
1	
2	
3	
4	
5	
6	
7	
8	
9	
10	

▼

BEHAVIORAL SIGNS FRAME

EVENT YOU ARE DESCRIBING	

Other of my behavioral signs that I can remember:

ANGER LEVEL	BEHAVIOR
1	
2	
3	
4	
5	
6	
7	
8	
9	
10	

▼

Other Behavioral Signs

Your own behavioral signs of anger are the ones most important to you, but it can be fun and instructive to look at other people's signs.

ASSIGNMENT 10

Directions:

1. Select at least five people. These can be people you know, people in the news, fictional characters, or television or movie characters. For each one, identify one or more behaviors that that person exhibits when he or she is angry. It will be easiest to identify people's behaviors when they are very angry, but also try to find some of the more subtle signs they show when they are just beginning to get angry. Use the following table to record your results. (If you need to, you can turn on the television set or postpone this assignment until tomorrow so that you can observe some people you know in real-life situations.)

PERSON	ANGER LEVEL	BEHAVIOR

▼

EFFECTIVE WAYS TO DEAL WITH ANGER

◄◄ **UNIT 1** ►►

GETTING ANGRY

Getting Angry—James' Way

It took James almost a week at the juvenile correctional institution before his caseworker felt it was "safe" to talk to him. In that time, James had discovered two things: he *really* wanted to get out of the institution, and he needed to change something about himself or he would spend a lot of his life in such places. These were the crucial discoveries that led James to turn his life around, although the path would not be an easy one.

It almost started out disastrously. Mr. Shields spent about two hours with James, going over the rules of the institution and getting to know the young man. It was obvious that James needed counseling to help him overcome his violent reactions to anger. By chance, I was assigned to be his counselor.

Our first session started much like Chapter 2 of this workbook. We chatted for a while, and then I asked James to describe an angry episode in his past, trying to recognize his physical signs as he did so. James wasn't ready to talk about the incident with Steven that had landed him in the institution, so he began to relate a different event.

"This guy I knew just got a car," James began. "It was a Chevy, 20 years old, full of rust and nothing much worked right, but he thought it was cool. He came around to where some of us were hanging out, turned his radio up loud, and leaned on his horn. We all just shouted at him to cut out the noise. But he just turned the radio up louder and did like this." (You will have to supply your own offensive gesture.)

"I probably would have let it go, but there was this girl I liked and she saw the whole thing. I had to do something." I stopped James at this point and asked him how his body felt at the time, but he said he didn't know. Then I told him to think back to the event and try to remember every detail. He proved to be very good at it. After pausing for a moment, he went on, his eyes far away.

"It was when I realized that Tricia was there that I got angry. I could feel my heart beating in my head, like a pulse. I even bit my own lip. I could taste the blood a little. Then I kicked at his fender, but all that did was hurt my foot. I didn't care about the pain. Then I grabbed his wiper blade and ripped it off. I was going to smash his window with it, but a couple of my friends grabbed me and held on."

"How did your body feel right then?" I asked. We had found two physical signs (the pounding head and the facial tension that led to his bitten lip) from when his anger began, but I wanted to discover some of his signs at the peak of anger. That would have to wait, however, because this time James surprised me.

"How do I know how?" he continued, obviously upset. "I'm being put down in front of my girl, my foot's nearly broken, and the wiper blade cut my hand. Do you think I care about my physical signs?" At this point, James ended the session by sweeping a couple of books and my notepad off the table.

What can we learn from James' account? The main thing is that James got angry very quickly. In the time between when he realized that Tricia was watching and when he kicked the fender, James only had time for two fleeting thoughts. When I asked him how he felt at the peak of his anger, he immediately shouted one sentence at me and then became physical (with the books and notepad). James went from 0 to 10 on the Anger Ruler with scarcely a heartbeat in between. Obviously, if we were going to find something to interrupt his anger cycle, it would have to work very quickly.

There are two other interesting things in this story. First, James revealed that he was very good at remembering and acting out his emotions. This would be of great help during later counseling. Second, James distorted the truth when he was angry. Did you notice how he referred to Tricia as "my girl" when he became angry at me? James readily admitted later that Tricia was not his girl; they had never gone out. He just thought she was "worth a look."

Getting Angry—Sharon's Way

If James could be said to have "the pedal to the metal" on the anger accelerator, Sharon would be like the driver who pokes her nose into traffic and then sits and looks around. Part of Sharon's therapy was to be open about herself with her friends. So we all got to hear a lot of her stories. This is one of them.

Sharon was not in an institution, but she needed help with her anger as much as James did. Luckily several of her friends were good listeners and empathic people. They were willing to help, but after listening to a few of her problems, they suggested that she see a counselor. At first, she said she didn't need one, but after a week or two it became obvious, even to Sharon, that she was not going to resolve her problem by herself.

After dinner one day, one of Sharon's friends asked her why it had taken her so long to get angry enough at Clark to do something. "They asked me that in therapy," she said, "and I first just said that I didn't know. It seemed as though something always came up—like this one time when we had been married for only a few months. I still looked up to Clark as a kind of hero. When he criticized me, I was sure it really was my fault.

"It was a Saturday night and we were going to go to the movies with friends. I was wearing a green dress I had bought that day, and I thought it looked good on me. Clark didn't like it, and, of course, he told me so. I felt pretty bad, but I just changed into the outfit I had worn the last weekend, which Clark seemed to like. But as soon as he saw me in it, he complained that if I wore the same thing every week, people would think we were poor.

"For the first time, I began to see through Clark a little. I glared at him and said: 'Well, *Mister* Clark, what do you think I should wear?' So he picked something out for me that really was far too dressy for a movie, but I put it on and didn't say anything. Actually, I said nothing to him for about half an hour—I just turned away and ignored him. Did Clark even notice? I doubt it.

"I might have been a *little* late getting ready, since I had to change twice, but Clark got very nasty and started yelling at me that we would miss the movie. I ignored him the first few times, but then I did start to get angry. When he called me a name, I stamped my foot on the floor a couple of times. Clark heard it and came right up to me. He said nothing, and I just pretended that nothing had happened.

"When we got to the movies, Clark really embarrassed me. He told our friends that he was sorry we were late, but it was because I never learned how to dress myself. I tried to make a joke out of it, but Clark kept on with his sarcasm. It really shocked me. It was one of those things that really change a relationship. I excused myself in a small voice, went to the restroom, and cried it out. It took me 20 minutes to get into the movie and find Clark and our friends. When I sat down, Clark didn't say a word."

She paused for a moment, and then concluded: "I might have done something right then, but he did offer me some of the popcorn, so I decided to just to let it drop."

It took a lot to get Sharon from 1 to even 3 or 4 on the Anger Ruler. Once she got there, she expressed herself very mildly, if at all. Do you think her anger quickly went back to 0? I doubt it. Sharon did not know how to let her anger dissipate. By the end of the evening, Sharon's anger had reached 9 or 10, but it had taken two hours to get there. The techniques Sharon would have to learn to use to deal with anger would be quite different from those that James would need.

Getting Angry—Your Way

Do you see a little of yourself in both James and Sharon? Most people fall somewhere between these two extremes. Go to a blank page in your notebook and write down some short answers to the questions in Assignment 11.

ASSIGNMENT 11

Directions:
1. How long does it usually take you to go from 1 to 10 on the Anger Ruler?
2. Do you always get all the way to 10? If not, where do you usually stop?
3. When your anger stopped far short of 10, what made you stop?
4. In those cases where your anger did get out of control, can you think of anything you might have done to stop it before it got to 10?

◄◄ UNIT 2 ►►
THE INTERVENTION MODEL

Recognize–Evaluate–Intervene

There are just several things you need to do in order to control your anger and make it serve you. I call the entire process the "Intervention Model." This chapter concerns the first three steps. When you have learned these three, you will be able to keep your anger under control. The rest of the Intervention Model will take you further than most people ever go by turning anger into a positive tool.

Of the three steps, you already know how to do the first one. The second is easy to learn and takes up only part of this unit. Since the rest of this chapter is devoted to step 3, you might think that it will be very difficult, but that's not the case. Actually, you will be offered a large number of techniques from which you can select the ones that best suit you.

The three steps are:

1. *Recognize that you are angry*. You learned how to do this in Chapter 2, and you are probably fairly good at it already. As you go through the rest of this workbook, you will become more and more proficient at recognizing anger signs in the earliest stages of your anger.
2. Quickly *evaluate the situation*. Are you in physical danger? Usually you are not, but if you are, treat this threat first. If there is no physical threat, or if you have already dealt with it, you know you are dealing with anger.
3. Intervene to *stop your anger from growing out of control*. "Intervene" means to do something that you are not doing now. The goal of the intervention is to put your logical mind back in charge.

Master these three steps and you usually will escape from an angry episode with little or no damage done. You will sit on that wild horse and not get thrown ignobly to the ground. In later chapters, you will learn how to unleash the power of your mind to do much more than just damage control. You will learn to truly tame the wild horse and make it go where you will. For this chapter, just remaining upright on the horse's back will be enough.

Evaluating the Situation

In step 1, you used your physical and behavioral signs to recognize an emotion that is anger or one of its close kin (fear or surprise). The next thing you must do is determine which emotion you are feeling and why.

This is something you do quite naturally. If a man is coming at you with a knife, you recognize the emotion (fear) and identify the threat (the man with the knife) almost without thinking. In fact, step 2 can be summarized in one simple question: "What is the threat?.

Surprise: There Is No Threat

If there is no threat at all, then you feel only surprise. Some adrenaline may be flowing and you may experience some of your anger signs, but you can tell right away that nothing is threatening you. In this case, what should you do? The answer is "nothing." You are only surprised—there is no threat—there is nothing to do.

Sometimes surprise turns to anger when there is no good reason for it to do so. In this case, you treat it just like anger, using the interventions presented in the rest of this chapter. But when you can, turn it off immediately: you are only surprised—there is no threat—there is nothing to do.

Fear: There Is a Physical Threat

If there is a physical threat to your survival or health, you are feeling fear. You may also be feeling anger at the same time. In this case, you must put anger aside and deal first with the physical threat. What if you are not able to do this? Once again, you use the interventions you will learn shortly to check your anger as quickly as possible. Then you turn your attention to the physical threat.

Exactly how you meet the physical threat depends on the nature of the threat and your own physical and mental abilities. Some of the problem-solving skills described in later chapters could help you. In general, the way you deal with physical threats is similar to the way in which you deal with emotional ones, so by the time you finish this workbook, you will be well equipped to handle both kinds. For now, just remember to isolate the physical threat and deal with it first.

Anger: There Is an Emotional Threat

Once you have recognized and dealt with your surprise and fear, whatever is left is truly anger. Anger is caused by a threat to your emotional well-being. You can probably identify this threat very exactly, if you try. Often it is a threat to your self-image—the way you see yourself or the way others see you. A man coming at you with a knife causes fear (the physical threat), but if your friends are watching, there is also anger. In our model, you deal with the physical threat first. This might mean running away. Once you have escaped the threat to your survival or health, you then deal with the anger.

SUMMARY:
Surprise—no threat—no action.
Fear—physical threat—address it first.
Anger—what's left—read on!

Unit 3 of this chapter introduces the interventions for anger, and the rest of the chapter deals with these interventions in detail.

ASSIGNMENT 12

Directions:

1. Think of any episode in your life when you felt surprised, fearful, or angry. If you prefer, use something you saw on television or in a movie. Fill in the following Event Table with the actions you feel you should have taken.

2. Repeat this exercise two or three times. Your counselor can give you more blank Event Tables, or you can just use pages in your notebook.

EVENT TABLE

1. Briefly describe the event.	
2. Was there any threat? Answer Yes or No.	
3. If there was a threat, was there a physical threat to your survival or health? If so, describe it.	
4. If there was no threat, what was your emotion? Hint: The answer is "surprise." If there was a threat, skip this question.	
5. If there was a survival threat, what was your emotion (hint: fear)? If there was no survival threat, skip this question.	
6. Was there a threat to your emotional well-being (anger)? If so, what was the threat? Note: You might feel both fear and anger.	
7. If there was fear, how should you have reacted to the physical threat?	
8. If there was anger, how did you keep it, or could you have kept it, under control?	

▼

◄◄ UNIT 3 ►►
ANGER-INTERRUPTION TECHNIQUES

You Have Come a Long Way

At this point, already you have learned how to recognize your anger and how to evaluate the threat that triggered the emotion. You know how the wild horse is going to buck. In the rest of this chapter, you will learn how to stay on the horse's back.

The ways in which you will learn to deal with anger are called Anger-Interruption Techniques, or AITs. You could also call them "skills," "strategies," or "tricks." Whatever you call them, AITs are used to control all three of the "anger demons":

- ▸ Angry feelings
- ▸ Angry thoughts
- ▸ Angry behaviors

How AITs Work

Each AIT is a skill that you can use by itself. Once you are comfortable with them, you will also be able to use combinations of AITs. In order for these techniques to be effective, it is very important that you practice each one until you feel you have mastered it. As with anything new, these techniques may seem strange at first, but as you practice, they become automatic, just like breathing. In fact, one of them *is* breathing.

Each AIT is based on the idea of *interrupting* the cycle of anger. By stopping your anger from growing beyond level 2 or 3 on the Anger Ruler, you make it much easier to control. This is what "interruption" is all about, and this is why the skills you will be learning are called Anger-*Interruption* Techniques.

The AIT Triangle

The AITs you will be learning are divided into three main groups:

- ▸ Relaxation techniques
- ▸ Self-talk and thought stopping
- ▸ Time-out techniques

You will learn relaxation techniques in Units 4, 5, and 6. Unit 7 deals with self-talk and thought stopping. Unit 8 describes time-out techniques, and Unit 9 pulls it all together. Assignment 13 will help you visualize how these three groups of AITs are different, and yet can all work together.

▼

ASSIGNMENT 13

Directions:

1. On a piece of paper or cardboard, draw a triangle. In the middle of the triangle, print "AITs." On one side of the triangle, write "Relaxation"; on another, write "Self-Talk/Thought Stopping"; and on the third, write "Time-Out." You can laminate this triangle if you wish.

2. Place your Anger Ruler on top of the AIT Triangle, as shown below. Of what does this remind you? It is meant to look like a scale, with the Anger Ruler balanced on the AIT Triangle. This is to remind you that you will learn to balance your anger using AITs.

3. Keep your AIT Triangle and Anger Rule handy.

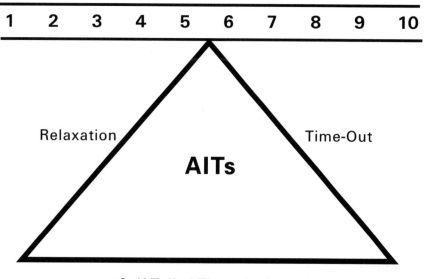

Figure 1. The Anger Ruler balanced on the AIT Triangle

◀◀ **UNIT 4** ▶▶

RELAXATION—BREATHING

The Opposite of "Tense"

In Chapter 2, you discovered the physical signs that indicated that you were angry. Even at early stages of anger, you probably noticed muscle tightness or rapid breathing. In short, you became tense. What is the opposite of tense? Think of an answer before reading the next paragraph.

There are several good answers, but the one I am looking for is "relaxed." Relaxation interrupts the physical process of anger. Just as it is impossible for a muscle to be both relaxed and tense at the same time, your mind cannot be both relaxed and tense simultaneously.

Let's look at it graphically. Your anger cycle starts out as in Figure 2, with anger leading to tension.

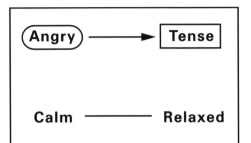

Figure 2. Anger leads to muscle tension.

By using one of the relaxation techniques you will learn in this unit and the next two units, you overcome your tension and become relaxed.

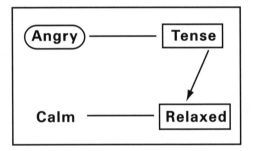

Figure 3. An AIT is used to change the tense state to a relaxed one.

Once you have relaxed your body and your mind, the anger cycle is broken and you become calm.

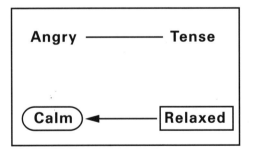

Figure 4. Relaxation leads to calm and interrupts the anger cycle.

Relaxation can take many forms. You can learn physical ways to relax your muscles and let your mind follow. Or you can relax your mind first and then your body will follow. There are different ways to learn how to relax physically, and there are different ways to relax your mind. In this unit, you will learn a way to relax your body.

Deep, Slow, Rhythmic Breathing

One of the easiest and quickest ways to relax your body is through *breathing*. You probably are thinking that you already know how to breathe. But the breathing that is an effective AIT is a special rhythmic kind of deep, slow breathing. Learning to breathe in this way relaxes your body, and interrupts the physical process of anger. The technique is very easy to learn.

Start by inhaling (taking air in) through your nose, very slowly, until you can feel your lungs filled with air. When you are comfortably full of air, exhale (breathe out) slowly. You may exhale through either your nose or your mouth, whichever you find more relaxing. The important thing is to inhale and exhale slowly and gently. Try it a few times.

When you inhale deeply, your chest and stomach expand, and when you exhale, they contract. As you practice deep breathing, watch your chest and stomach. They are good indicators of how deep your breaths are. You may feel like yawning when you first start breathing deeply. That's quite normal.

It is important to develop a steady rhythm with your deep breathing. If you breathe deeply too rapidly, you can hyperventilate, and even become dizzy. Obviously, this is not relaxation. If you breathe too slowly, you will simply become out of breath, so you will know you need to breathe a little faster. What you want to do is establish a steady rhythm, breathing in and out at the same pace, time after time.

Not only do you want to breathe at a steady pace, but you also want to breathe in and out at the same rate. It is not relaxing to inhale quickly and exhale slowly, or vice versa. Try it. Breathe in very quickly and then breathe out slowly. That's not what you want to do. Now do the opposite—breathe in very slowly and then exhale rapidly. That's not right either.

In Assignment 14, you will be asked to practice deep rhythmic breathing. Here are a few tricks that may help you get the most out of this technique

- Before you start, assume a comfortable position. This may be sitting or lying down.
- If you wish, close your eyes.
- To make sure that you are breathing at a steady pace, you can try counting while you breathe, starting each breath at 1. If, for example, you count to 6 with each breath, you should be inhaling for 1, 2, 3 and exhaling for 4, 5, 6. If you prefer, use a sentence or a song instead of counting.

ASSIGNMENT 14

Directions:

1. Practice deep rhythmic breathing. Try it for a minute or two.

2. Now try it again, this time making sure that your breaths are coming at a steady rate.

3. What method did you use (counting, singing, saying a sentence in your head, etc.) to time your breaths? Practice again, using different methods until you find one that you like.

4. To make sure that you are not inhaling faster than you are exhaling or exhaling faster than you are inhaling, practice one more time. Count forward while you are inhaling (1, 2, 3 ,4) and then backwards while you exhale (4, 3, 2, 1).

5. Imagine yourself in a stressful situation—either a real event or an imaginary one. Visualize your reactions and your feelings. Let your stress or anger build up until it reaches about a 7 on the Anger Ruler and then start your rhythmic breathing. How long does it take you to lose your stress?

6. Put it all together for one longer session (at least four or five minutes) of deep rhythmic breathing. While you are doing this, notice how your body feels. Compare this with what you wrote down in Assignment 4. Have you found some new physical signs of calmness? If you did, write them down on Assignment 4's Physical Signs Frame.

The Many Uses of Deep Breathing

It is important that you practice breathing exercises every day. Once you have learned this technique, you can begin to use it to relax at any time and in any place. For example, if you feel as though you are getting anxious during a test, try your breathing technique.

ASSIGNMENT 15

Directions:

1. In the Stressful Incidents Table that follows, list five times when deep rhythmic breathing to help you relax might be useful. Some examples (but don't use these) are in a traffic jam, when you bang your knee accidentally on a door, or when these assignments get on your nerves.

STRESSFUL INCIDENTS TABLE

1	
2	
3	
4	
5	

Practice Makes Perfect

One of the objections to deep breathing as an AIT is that it doesn't work quickly enough. You may be overwhelmed by your anger before you can use it. The answer to this objection is "practice." The more often you use deep breathing, the more quickly it will work for you. You may reach the point where one or two breaths are all that you need to achieve a reasonable degree of calmness! For this reason, you should use deep breathing frequently, whenever a situation arises that stresses you. It will soon become a habit. The effort that you put into practice will pay off.

Relaxation = Control!

Once you have reached the point with deep breathing (or any other relaxation technique) that you can use it whenever you want, you will have accomplished much more than just stopping anger. Relaxation is your personal cue telling you that you are in control. When you are relaxed, you think clearly and quickly, you see your options, and you make good choices. Your body also functions efficiently, letting you carry out the choices made by your mind.

When a basketball player goes to the free-throw line, he or she relaxes and concentrates. The relaxed state improves eye–hand coordination, and allows the body to perform its task with control. If you have a basketball court available, try tensing all your muscles and then shooting a free throw. Most likely it will be a brick (for those who don't play basketball, "shooting a brick" is not a desirable thing to do).

> **SUMMARY:** It's really as simple as 1–2–3: deep rhythmic breathing–relaxation–control.

◄◄ UNIT 5 ►►
MUSCLE RELAXATION

Deep breathing is a great AIT, but there are other ways to relax your body that go beyond inhaling and exhaling. One such method is *muscle relaxation*. It has most of the beneficial effects of deep breathing and is just as easy to learn.

The Fist

Can you tell a tense muscle from a relaxed one? Let's find out by experimenting with your fist. Clench your fist as hard as you can for about five seconds. Then slowly release it. What were the differences between a clenched fist and a relaxed fist? Try clenching and unclenching your fist a few times and then answer the question.

Let's see if you noticed all of these differences:
▸ Appearance of the muscles. Clench your fist; notice how the muscles look. Unclench it. Did you see the difference?

▶ Feel of the muscles. This time, when you clench your fist, touch the tense muscles and see how they feel. Do the same with the relaxed fist.

▶ Now close your eyes and clench your fist. How does it feel? Notice the various sensations, such as pressure, pain, and tautness. How do these differ from the sensations you experience when you unclench it?

You are now going to do an assignment in which you will discover the difference between how other muscles feel when they are tense and when they are relaxed. To start this assignment, find a quiet, comfortable place. You can sit on a comfortable chair or lie down on your bed. Make sure you are not putting stress on any part of your body. For example, do not cross your legs or your arms, since this puts pressure on those body parts.

If you are sitting, place both feet on the ground and let your arms rest gently on your thighs. If you are lying down, allow your legs and arms to rest naturally. Make sure that you are sitting or lying freely without any obstructions putting physical stress on your body. In short, see how comfortable you can get.

ASSIGNMENT 16

Directions:

1. For each part of the body listed below, first tense it and then relax it. Notice the difference in appearance, feel, and sensation. Repeat this exercise at least two or three times for each body part.

  a. Toes on your right foot. (Hint: Wiggle your toes first to identify the muscles.)

  b. Right ankle. (Hint: To feel the tension, touch the back of the ankle.)

  c. Toes on your left foot.

  d. Left ankle.

  e. Both ankles together. (Extra credit: Can you tense your ankles while keeping your toes relaxed?)

  f. Left calf (muscle between your knees and ankles). (Hint: If you are having trouble identifying or tensing the calf muscle, stand on your toes—it will be easy to see.)

  g. Right calf.

  h. Either calf, but make sure that all other muscles in your leg are relaxed.

2. The important thing to remember is that by initially tensing each muscle in your body and then relaxing it, you will learn to recognize the difference between a tense muscle and a relaxed muscle. Some muscles may be more difficult to isolate and tense, such as the smaller muscles, so you may need to practice longer on these muscles. Now continue with the exercise.

  i. Upper leg muscles.

  j. Stomach.

  k. Left hand.

  l. Right hand.

  m. Left arm.

n. Right arm.

o. Shoulders and neck.

3. The muscles of your face and head can get very tense almost without your knowing it. Continue this exercise by tensing and relaxing these muscles

p. Forehead.

q. Eyes (Hint: Shutting your eyes very tight is a good way to tense these muscles)

r. Ears.

s. Jaw.

4. Some people say that the key to relaxing the face muscles is the tongue. Try relaxing your *tongue*. Notice that many other facial muscles relax along with it.

COMMENTS ON ASSIGNMENT 16

When you have finished this exercise, you will be able to tell the difference between a relaxed muscle and a tense one. It will not be necessary for you to tense muscles any longer in order to relax them, because you can now recognize the tension and go directly to a relaxed state. Of course, whenever you are having difficulty trying to relax a muscle, you can always fall back on tensing the muscle first.

The AIT for muscle relaxation is simple. Whenever you recognize anger, notice which muscles are tense. Then relax them. In a short time, you will learn which of your muscles are most likely to become tense during anger and you can concentrate on them.

SPECIAL ASSIGNMENT

Directions:

1. This special assignment is not mandatory and does not deal specifically with anger, but you might find it fun. This is a particularly good assignment to do with your counselor. Now that you have learned both deep breathing and muscle relaxation, you can combine them to put yourself in such a relaxed state that you may even fall asleep! To do this, first assume a very comfortable sitting-up or lying-down position. If you like, have soothing music playing in the background.

Read the rest of this assignment and then do what it says. Begin doing deep rhythmic breathing. When you have established this rhythm, start relaxing your muscles, one at a time. Go back over them and make sure that some of them didn't tense up again as you concentrated on others. Once you have all of your muscles relaxed, concentrate on your breathing, keeping it deep, slow, and steady. Some people like to count the breaths, keeping all other thoughts out of their minds. You can continue this exercise as long as you wish. Even if you don't fall asleep (most people don't), you will probably feel very refreshed when you are finished.

> When you are in a very relaxed state, you may notice that some of your senses are especially acute. You can try concentrating on your hearing. Can you isolate sounds that normally you wouldn't even notice?

◀◀ **UNIT 6** ▶▶

RELAXING IMAGERY

Thoughts Can Get in the Way

Sometimes, when you are trying to relax, your thoughts may get in the way. That was one of the problems James had. His first few weeks in the institution were very difficult. Counseling progressed slowly, he made no friends, and the staff was not particularly pleasant to him. The main cause of his problems was his temper, but although James learned to identify his anger very early in its cycle, he was having trouble doing anything about it.

Typical was an incident in the dining hall. James thought that one of the other boys had bumped into him on purpose and he began to get angry. He realized what was happening, correctly identified the emotion as anger, and even started deep breathing. But after three or four breaths, he lost control and hurled the other boy's plate against a not-so-nearby wall. This did nothing to endear him further to the staff members, who responded by locking James in a punishment room.

At the next therapy session, we talked about what had happened. James told me that the deep breathing was working, but he kept thinking about how the other boy was trying to "test" him. He couldn't get that thought out of his head and this caused him to lose control. Clearly, James needed another tool in his relaxation tool box. Fortunately, there was one ideally suited to the task.

Introducing "Relaxing Imagery"

The relaxation process can often be greatly aided by using what we call *relaxing imagery*. Relaxing imagery refers to having pleasant pictures in your mind. This can be an imaginary trip or simply a peaceful, pleasant image. Like James, we will start with the pleasant-image technique, which is easy to learn and can be put to use immediately.

You are going to close you eyes and imagine a peaceful, calm setting. The first thing to do is to pick the image. Here are some possibilities.

- ▶ A cool forest
- ▶ A warm beach
- ▶ Mountains
- ▶ A green valley
- ▶ A gentle waterfall
- ▶ A slow-flowing river or creek

▸ A peaceful lake

▸ Snow or rain

Choose one of these if any appeal to you, or think of a different one. Assignment 17 makes use of your choice of image.

ASSIGNMENT 17

Directions:

1. Read this entire paragraph before beginning. Assume a comfortable sitting position or lie down on your bed. Make sure that you are not stressing any part of your body (legs not crossed, arms resting easily at your sides, etc.). Begin slow, deep breathing. Relax all of your muscles. When you are fully relaxed, imagine the image you have chosen. You may close your eyes, if you like. While keeping the image in mind, notice how relaxed your mind and body are. Continue this for a minute or two. Do this step now and then go on to the next direction.

2. Do the same thing again. Now it should take you less time to get to the relaxed state. As you see your relaxing image, bring all five senses into play and remember what you sense. When you are finished, write down your reactions in the Sensory Table.

SENSORY TABLE

SENSE	YOUR IMPRESSION
Sight	
Smell	
Hearing	
Touch	
Taste	

James Experiences a Major Success

James chose a forest scene as his image. He went through the exercise you just completed, but told me afterwards he did not see how this would help him "out there." However, it did.

During the next week, James was sorely provoked by a staff member who was tired of James' tantrums. The other boys were going to dinner, but James was held back because he was told to return to his room to put on a clean shirt. As usual, James began to get angry, but he took a couple of deep breaths and managed to calm down. The staff noticed the signs that, in the past, had signaled angry outbursts from James and warned him: "Go off now and you don't get dinner at all."

At our next session, James told me how he reacted. "I hate it when they get on me like that. And I wasn't even going to do anything. It wasn't fair. But I knew that if I reacted, I wouldn't get dinner, and I was hungry. So I remembered the forest scene, and I just relaxed my fists and took a real deep breath and made it come into my mind."

A look of pride came into James' eyes. I could see his shoulders straighten, and, as he continued, he looked right at me (which was unusual for James). "Well, it worked. In just a second or two, I could feel the anger leave my head. It couldn't stay in there with all those tall green trees."

He seemed to be seeing the trees again, and he said nothing more. We sat there silently for a few moments, both of us enjoying his triumph. "So what happened?" I asked finally. "Oh," James concluded, "not much. I didn't say anything. I just changed my shirt and came back down. Mr. Riggs (the staff member) looked surprised. He didn't hassle me any more on the way to the dining hall—he even told me to hurry up because they were having fried chicken."

This was the first time that James had been able to use AITs to shut down his anger. From that time on, his attitude toward counseling was very positive because he knew that what we were doing was working. As you apply what we have learned to your life, you will make the same discovery.

SUMMARY: This stuff really works!

An Advanced Course

James had done so well with the relaxing image that we went on to a more involved technique, using an entire imaginary journey.

Starting with a relaxing image (you may use the same one as before or pick a new one), you relax and imagine a journey beginning with that image. I will describe such a journey for you shortly. But before we start, there is one more trick of relaxing that I want to introduce.

A Point on the Ceiling

In the past, when you did your relaxation exercises, you sat or lay down, did deep breathing, and relaxed your muscles. You may have closed your eyes to help you avoid distractions. There is another way in which you can achieve the concentration we are seeking. If this way works better for you, use it. If not, forget it.

Pick an imaginary target straight ahead of you—a point on the wall, if you are sitting, or on the ceiling, if you are lying down. Look at this target as you achieve rhythmic breathing. As you relax your muscles and continue breathing, you will find that the area surrounding your imaginary target is becoming dark, and your focus is narrowing down to that target. You may have experienced this before —some people call it "spacing out." What is really going on is that you are focusing closely somewhere else. In this case, the imaginary target is the focus of your concentration.

As the process continues, you will find that your eyes seem to be relaxing. Some people have reported that the wall containing their imaginary target seems to move. This is probably because their eyes are beginning to get tired, and the shadows playing against the wall may make the wall look as if it is moving. When this happens, feel free to close your eyes and continue your relaxation.

There is no formal assignment for this technique, but you should try it now to see if it will be useful to you in achieving a relaxed state.

Your Relaxing Journey

In Assignment 18, you are going to take a relaxing journey, starting at a peaceful image that you choose. To give you an idea of what this journey is supposed to be like, take a look at what James wrote about in his journey. (James would surprise his old friends in more ways than one—he turned out to be a good writer, and even a bit of a poet.) Here is James' description of his journey.

I see in front of me a dense forest, with very tall trees. As I enter the forest, I find myself walking very lightly over a soft, green, mossy path. The moss under my feet feels soft and cushiony, giving me the sensation of floating. I am weightless, walking and floating down the path, the soft warm coolness cushioning the soles of my feet. My feet relax, enjoying for themselves the cool warmth, and my body becomes ever lighter.

I hear the gentle music of the leaves rustling softly in the wind. The sounds are familiar; I even recognize the tune. The cool breeze caresses my skin, and I allow myself to be guided forward by its gentleness. I am amazed at the different colors of the leaves, colors that I never imagined could be so bright and bold. The forest is full of earth scents. The mint smell is so subtle but also so strong that I can almost taste it. It is both cool and energizing at the same time. I also smell the sweet caramel of the bark of graceful ponderosa pine, and the taste of an ice cream sundae forms in my mouth.

ASSIGNMENT 18

Directions:

1. Read this entire assignment before beginning it. Decide on the image you are going to use to start your journey.

2. Sit down or lie down and enter a relaxed state by doing deep breathing and muscle relaxation. You may use the imaginary-target skill if you wish.

3. When you feel completely relaxed, bring up your starting image. Allow a story to unfold any way it wants to. Make sure you continue to breathe deeply throughout your journey.

4. Take your time and enjoy your trip. When it is time to return, remember to bring back with you a smell, a taste, a sight, a sound, and a touch.

5. Fill out the Sensory Table about your journey. Or, you prefer, write a narrative about it similar to the one that James wrote.

SENSE	YOUR IMPRESSION
Sight	
Smell	
Hearing	
Touch	
Taste	

COMMENTS ON ASSIGNMENT 18

You can try a couple of variations on this assignment.

If you find a partner to help you, ask him or her to provide the story. Your partner should speak slowly in a soothing, low voice, giving you time to experience each moment along the way. Your counselor can also do this with you.

You can also record the journey on a tape recorder and play it back while you are in a relaxed state.

SUMMARY: You now know three AITs—deep breathing, muscle relaxation, and relaxing imagery. Select the best parts of each and use them in your life. Remember the three steps:

Recognize your anger.

Identify the threat.

Use an AIT to regain control.

▼

◄◄ UNIT 7 ►►
SELF-TALK AND THOUGHT STOPPING

Cheerleaders Are Not Always "Cheery"

A pretty girl with long blonde hair, she was sitting quietly on a bench. She seemed absorbed by the cheerleading team practicing in the nearby field. Her eyes had a faraway look, as though they were focused on the cheerleaders. She watched as they practiced. The cheerleaders, unaware of the girl on the bench, laughed, danced, and practiced their routines. They did not notice her. They did not notice that she was not dancing or laughing.

The girl sat there quietly with her quiet thoughts. "Look at them," she thought. "They think they are so important, and so beautiful. They probably think I'm a loser. But it's not my fault that I'm not on the team. The judges didn't like me because I'm not as beautiful as the other girls…they probably hate me…I'll get even one of these days—just watch."

As the team finished practicing, the cheerleaders walked by the bench where the girl sat, but still no one seemed to notice her. As the sun started to set, the quiet girl got up, and started walking home. "Just you wait," she thought, as she felt her heart beating fast, her hands getting sweatier, and her eyes beginning to tear.

What do you think is happening with this girl? What is she doing? What do you think she might end up doing?

Right! It Was Self-Talk

What the blonde girl was doing is called "self-talk." In conjunction with *thought stopping*, self-talk is an AIT that can accelerate anger or control it. Self-talk refers to the messages that you give yourself in any situation. In an angry or unpleasant type of situation, there are likely to be more negative thoughts than positive thoughts, and probably more negative self-talk. For example, what do you tell yourself when you have just received an award? You probably do not actually talk to yourself (although some people do), but you might have a personal thought, such as, "I did a good job, and I feel great about it."

When you make a mistake, however, the messages you send yourself are a bit different.

Self-talk can either increase or decrease the intensity of a feeling, depending on how you use it. Negative self-talk (such as "I really messed up this time," or "I'm really stupid," or "It's not my fault, they're being unfair") usually makes you feel worse, and accomplishes very little other than deepening your anger.

Now you can recognize what the blonde girl was doing. She was having an internal dialog or self-talk that was leading her to an angrier and angrier state.

▼

ASSIGNMENT 19

Directions:

1. Get out your Anger Ruler. In the following Angry Statement Table, the girl's self-talk is listed on the left. In the right-hand column, write the number on the Anger Ruler that you think corresponds to each of her statements.

ANGRY STATEMENT TABLE

STATEMENT	ANGER VALUE
"They think they are so important and so beautiful."	
"They probably think I'm a loser."	
"The judges didn't like me because I'm not as beautiful as the other girls."	
"They probably hate me."	
"I'll get even one of these days."	

COMMENTS ON ASSIGNMENT 19

This pattern of increasing anger values shows that the girl's anger was accelerating. Her negative self-talk appears to be the cause.

It is important to notice that the girl was doing all this in her head, and that the cheerleading team did not do anything to contribute to her self-talk. This kind of self-talk led the blonde girl to start experiencing physical signs of anger. Would she act on her anger? That depends on a lot of other factors. For example, if she were to read the rest of this unit, she would have the skill to interrupt her anger cycle.

Changing Directions

Positive self-talk, on the other hand, can change the direction of anger. But how could the blonde girl turn her negative self-talk into positive self-talk?

It turns out to be as simple as what you do when you find yourself driving backwards when the door to the garage is in front of you. First you say to yourself, "Oops." Then you hit the brakes to stop the car, shift gears, tap on the gas, and begin to go in the right direction. With negative self-talk, the steps are analogous:

▸ Realize that you are engaging in negative self-talk.

▸ Stop it.

▸ Get yourself "into gear" with positive self-talk.

The first step is easy; you will not have much trouble realizing that what you are saying to yourself is negative. The second step is called "thought stopping."

Thought Stopping

Thought stopping is an important way of interrupting negative thoughts. You can stop a negative thought by doing something as simple as counting. You may have heard the old saying, "If angry, count to 10; if very angry, count to 100." There is a certain wisdom in this; counting will interrupt negative thoughts. It also provides you with a mental "time-out" — but that's Unit 8!

An even simpler way is this. Whenever you get a negative thought, force yourself to see an image in your mind. You can pick any image that has meaning for you, but a few common choices are:

▸ A stop sign.

▸ A red light.

▸ The word "STOP" or "NO" on a television screen.

The important thing is to focus your attention on this image. You will have to practice it the next few times you begin to experience negative self-talk, but it will soon become your own "mental brake."

Some people prefer a physical action instead of a mental image. For example, you might take a few deep breaths, or you might shake you head like a dog shaking water off of its coat.

Take a few moments to come up with a sign that you find comfortable. Try some of the ones listed above and make up a few of your own. Then choose one that you think will work for you. From now on, whenever you find yourself engaging in negative self-talk, use your mental brake.

Make It Positive

So far you have accomplished the first two steps we listed under "Changing Directions." You have stopped the acceleration of your anger caused by negative self-talk by stopping the self-talk. But you can do more. Let's go on to the third step — positive self-talk.

Let's say that the blonde girl did know about self-talk and was able to apply her mental brake. The self-conversation might now take a different turn

The girl sat on the bench with her quiet thoughts. "Look at them," she thought. "They think they are so important, and so beautiful. They probably think I'm a loser. But it's not my fault that I'm not on the team. The judges didn't like me because I'm not as beautiful as the other girls…they probably hate me…I'll get even one of these days—just watch."

As the team finished practicing, the cheerleaders walked by the bench where the girl sat, but still no one seemed to notice her. As the sun started to set, the girl suddenly realized that she had been engaging in negative self-talk, and that she was getting very angry. She formed an image of a police officer in an old movie blowing his whistle to command a thief to stop.

This applied her mental brake and interrupted her anger cycle. But she still felt pretty low. If she had finished this unit, she would have known how to turn a negative into a positive, like this: "I know why I didn't make the cheerleading team—I didn't practice enough. Those girls are good at the routines. But I can be just as good—even better. I'll just watch the team for a few days and learn the routines. Then I'll practice. When the tryouts come around again next season, nothing will keep me off the team."

In this way, the girl actually would do more than just turn her negative self-talk into positive self-talk. She also would develop a plan to avoid the problem in the future. She was engaged in problem solving, which you will learn about in a later chapter. However, if this kind of positive self-talk comes naturally to you, by all means use it.

ASSIGNMENT 20

Directions:

1. Imagine a situation in which you might get angry and engage in negative self-talk. In the following Self-Talk Table, write a few sentences of this negative self-talk.

2. Fill in the image or action that is your mental brake.

3. Now fill in some positive self-talk in which you could engage after applying your mental brake.

SELF-TALK TABLE

Negative self-talk	
Mental brake	
Positive self-talk	

▼

◀◀ UNIT 8 ▶▶
TIME-OUTS

Counting to 10

Time-outs are one of the simplest and most effective of the Anger-Interruption Techniques. Timing yourself out means giving yourself "time out" from a situation long enough to think about alternatives. In a way, a time-out is like thought stopping because it interrupts the anger cycle. But a time-out goes a step further. It gives you a specific amount of time during which you decide not to react further to whatever it was that was making you angry.

The most famous of the time-out techniques is "counting to 10." Half of the mothers in the world have told their children, "When you get angry, count to 10." (The other half wish they had!) Of course, counting to 10 is not just a time-out. It causes you to interrupt your anger and gives you time to cool off.

A Time-Out Is More Than Just "Time Out"

However, there is much more than this to time-outs. As you begin to understand the power of this AIT, you will appreciate how much you can do with such a simple strategy. A time-out is an effective *self-message*. When you time yourself out, you are giving yourself the message that you are in control and that you can take care of yourself. A time-out also gives you time to evaluate your alternatives and to pick the one that will do you the most good.

SUMMARY: The three powers of time-outs are:

1. They interrupt the anger cycle.

2. They tell you that you are in control.

3. They give you time to think of your choices.

That's not bad for just counting to 10.

Physical Time-Outs

A physical time-out is an action that physically removes you from an angry or threatening situation. Turning away or walking out of a room is a physical time-out. Sometimes just shutting your eyes is sufficient. Other physical time-outs are going for a walk, running, riding a bicycle, listening to music, or reading.

Some of these techniques are more suitable for when you are very angry or your anger is accelerating rapidly. The one that can be used in almost all situations is walking away. Other techniques can be used effectively when you need to overcome a continuing irritant, but one that does not threaten to cause you immediately to lose control.

For example, if someone is taunting you in front of your friends, walking away will work, but reading a book is not likely to help (unless it's a book about karate). However, if you are getting upset because a person who promised to meet you is very late, then listening to music or reading could be a very effective time-out.

The physical time-outs described here have one thing missing—a timer. Time-outs should last at least a certain predetermined length of time. Most physical time-outs do not have such a timer (an exception would be to take five deep breaths). Therefore, you need to devise one. If you walk away, make an agreement with yourself that you will not come back for at least one minute, or two minutes, or some other specific interval of time. If you are going to listen to music, decide to listen to a certain number of songs.

Thomas' Timer

A friend, Thomas Gunn (no one ever calls him "Tommy"), becomes very irritated whenever he finds himself in a line. Particularly difficult for him is waiting for a table at a restaurant. He fidgets and complains. Sometimes he even gets nasty. His favorite trick is saying, "Let's go somewhere else," but if you ask him "where," he never has an answer.

Once five of us, including Thomas, decided to go out to dinner. When we arrived at the restaurant, we were told that our table would be ready in about 15 or 20 minutes. Everyone looked at Thomas and began to get nervous. They say "necessity is the mother of invention," so I had to think of something. "Look," I said to Thomas, "I know waiting bothers you, but we're all having a good time talking, so just cool it. If they haven't called us in 20 minutes, let me know."

I had literally set Thomas a timer. He took out his pocket watch and stared at it for 17 minutes. Luckily, the hostess told us our table was ready before the 20 minutes were up.

Thomas' timer gave him a focus so that he could control his anxiety, which often resulted in angry behaviors. I don't know whether or not it helped him feel better, but it definitely kept him quiet!

Mental Time-Outs

There are also a number of time-outs that are mental instead of physical. Counting to 10 is a mental time-out. Others are naming all of the states (if you are one of the few who knows them all), singing a song to yourself, and reciting the alphabet backwards. Mental time-outs usually have their own built-in timers, so long as you don't cheat and do something like sing only the first line of your song.

Mental time-outs can be used when you cannot take a physical time-out. A private in the army being "ridden hard" by his sergeant cannot walk away, but can mentally count to 10.

ASSIGNMENT 21

Directions:

1. On a blank piece of paper in your notebook, list at least five time-out techniques that you think you could actually use in a situation in which you were getting angry quickly.

Practicing Time-Outs

This is how you practice taking time-outs. Whenever you recognize one of your anger signs, stop, say to yourself, "I need a time-out" (which is positive self-talk, by the way), and pick one of the time-out techniques that you listed in Assignment 21. Use that technique and see how effective it is for you. If it doesn't work well, discard it and choose some other technique. You will rapidly zero in on those particular time-outs that work for you.

If you happen to be with other people when you decide to take a time-out, see if you can tell them that you are only "taking a break." This is not always possible, but it will explain your behavior and make it easier for you when you want to return.

Time-Out Versus Running Away

It is important to be able to tell the difference between a time-out and avoiding dealing with problems. A time-out gives you an opportunity to sort out your feelings and thoughts and to plan your behavior. It gives you a chance to explore the meaning you gave the event, the feelings that resulted from this meaning, and the thoughts that might be contributing to the anger. This is different from running away from problems. When you run away from a problem, the problem remains, and it is just a matter of time until the same conflict and resulting feelings arise again. Time-outs are *not* running away.

◄◄ UNIT 9 ►►
PUTTING IT ALL TOGETHER

Using Your Anger Journal

As you can see, all of the AITs are related. The main purpose of these techniques is to allow you to maintain control so that you can focus on problem solving instead of just feeling miserable. By this time, you have learned about a large number of possible strategies; you probably like some of them better than others.

During the next weeks and months, as you work through the rest of this book, never forget the Intervention Model:
- ▸ Recognize your anger.
- ▸ Evaluate the situation ("What's the threat?").
- ▸ Do an AIT.

Have you forgotten your anger journal? Remember that you were going to record your angry experiences in it.
- ▸ The time when and the place where you became angry.
- ▸ What made you angry—what you were feeling and thinking.

▸ What you did when you became angry.

▸ The consequences of your angry behavior .

It is important for you to go back to keeping this journal current. Now that you have learned about AITs, you can also record a fifth item:

▸ The AIT you used and how well it worked.

Preparing Your AIT List

It is a good idea to have a few AITs "ready to go" for whenever you need them on short notice. Of the many possibilities you learned in Units 4 through 8, some will work better for you than others. For the next assignment, review your work in these units and pick several AITs for further testing.

When you do this, notice that some AITs are more useful at beginning stages of anger, whereas others may be used even when you are very angry. You know about different levels of anger (bring out your Anger Ruler to remind yourself), and you know how to recognize the anger signs that go with each level. Now you will also have AITs for each.

ASSIGNMENT 22

Directions:

1. Select at least five AITs that you think might work well for you. Choose at least one relaxation AIT, one self-talk AIT, and one time-out AIT. Be very specific—for example, don't just choose "time-out"; instead, specify "humming the *Star Spangled Banner* in my head."

2. Write each AIT on your AIT Triangle.

3. For each AIT, figure out for which anger levels on your Anger Ruler it would work. On the AIT Triangle, write the levels next to the AIT.

Pat Yourself on the Back

You have now completed the longest and probably the hardest chapter in this workbook. You have the skills to tame that "wild horse" of anger. You can get on the horse's back and not be thrown off. This is a very big accomplishment.

Of course, you are not perfect yet. There will probably be incidents that you will handle less successfully than you would like. That wild horse still has a few unexpected moves to show you. Never be discouraged by one incident—if the horse throws you, just get right back on. After all, he now has one less trick that you don't know about.

The rest of this book has two important objectives: to give you practice so that you can sharpen your skills, and to teach you how to harness the power of your anger (to make the wild horse carry you where you want to go).

▼

CHAPTER 4

EXPRESSING ANGER

◄◄ UNIT 1 ►►

INTRODUCTION

The Value of Bad Examples

This chapter is about the different ways in which people express or experience anger. Actually, it is about ways that do *not* work well. Why should you read about behaviors that *don't* work? See if you can come up with a reason before reading the next paragraph.

The reason is that this chapter will help you discover some of your own behaviors that need to be changed. Simply being aware of these destructive behaviors will help you to avoid them.

The "Fearsome" Five

Each of the next five units deals with one type of angry expression that you should avoid. In each unit, you will meet someone who represents an extreme case of a person using that type of behavior. As you read about them, see if you recognize any of your behaviors.

Here are the five categories of angry behaviors to avoid.
- Holding anger in.
- Escalating anger.
- Displacing anger (expressing anger at someone or something not related to the source of anger).
- Responding aggressively.
- Using drugs or alcohol.

It Is YOUR Responsibility!

It is important to keep in mind that what people do when they are angry is *entirely their responsibility*.

Take Mitchell, who got angry at his brother for being friendly with someone Mitchell didn't like. What did Mitchell do? He sucker-punched his brother in the gut. What did his brother do? He cracked Mitchell on the head with a handy lamp. Then both of them said: "Gee, I'm sorry, but I was angry." Great excuse, right? We have Mitchell with a cut on his head, his brother with a sore midsection, and a lamp that suffered a premature death. But it's all okay, because Mitchell and his brother were angry. Right?

Wrong. There are many situations in life that lead to strong feelings. These situations may catch people off guard because of how strongly they feel. However, people can and do learn to control their responses in terms of what they feel, what they think, and how they act in those situations. If they don't, being angry is no excuse for their behavior.

Unlike some of the people in the stories you will read in the following units, you *do* have the skills to halt undesirable angry behaviors. Your goals for this chapter are to:

> ▸ Identify those angry behaviors that you want to change.
> ▸ Learn to stop these behaviors before they hurt you or others.

◀◀ UNIT 2 ▶▶
STUFFING ANGER

The first behavior that you may recognize in yourself is "stuffing anger."

Stuffing anger means holding the angry feeling inside of you rather than doing something to make the feeling or the situation any better. Sharon is a perfect example of someone who stuffed her anger. She did not realize the extent or intensity of her anger. Holding anger in was a way in which she dealt with her ongoing poor relationship with her abusive husband.

Sharon Opens Up

It really was "a dark and rainy night." Thunder rumbled in the background. I was sitting in Sharon's living room with a group of our mutual friends. It seemed at first that the weather was the opposite of how Sharon described herself — she was quiet, self-effacing, and even meek. But we quickly learned that the real Sharon was much more like the storm than we had ever guessed.

On this evening, Sharon focused on the effects that stuffing her anger had on her. "I never really understood," she began, "what holding all of that anger in was doing to me. In fact, I didn't realize I *was* holding it in until that evening when I threw the spaghetti at Clark. In that one terrible and wonderful moment, I saw what had been happening to me for years. I felt a deep despair, both then and for the next few days. But gradually the despair went away and was replaced by hope. I think the reason for the hope was that each day I felt better and better."

Sharon looked at us in what seemed like amazement. If she was waiting for a response from us, she wasn't going to get one. This was her turn. We were still not completely used to hearing Sharon discuss her emotions. We understood how Sharon was using this openness to help assure herself that she would not bottle up her anger again.

Sharon continued. "I had held my anger in for so long that it had become a constant burden. It took its toll on me, both physically and emotionally. I was sad almost all of the time. I thought I wasn't good enough for anyone, not even Clark. I had a terrible pain in my neck."

"Yeah," one of her friends quipped, "it was Clark." Sharon laughed, too; it was good to see her laugh for a change. "Yes, he was, but I mean a real pain in my neck. My neck muscles were always so tense that they hurt. A heating pad didn't even help. My jaw muscles were so tense that my dentist told me that I was wearing my teeth down because I was grinding them so hard in my sleep.

"You can't imagine all of my physical symptoms. That stomach pain I had, which we thought was indigestion, turned out to be the beginning of an ulcer.

"After confronting Clark and deciding to leave, I started to feel better each day—not just mentally, but also physically. I noticed my muscles starting to relax, and the burning sensation in my stomach became less frequent. That's probably what gave me hope. My body was starting to recover physically, even though everything else was certainly bad enough—the money problems, having to tell my family, not even knowing where I was going to live. I realized how much better I was able to handle these other problems without having to battle the physical pain caused by the smoldering anger I felt toward Clark."

A Case of Dirty Laundry

Why do people stuff anger? Some may choose to hold anger in because they are afraid to confront their feelings or of what they might do if they allowed the anger to surface. These people think that they can lock the anger away inside themselves. However, the anger is still there, especially if the situation that causes the anger has not been resolved, as in Sharon's case. The result is physical and emotional pain.

Holding anger in is like stuffing dirty laundry into a bag. You may not see the dirty clothes when they are in the bag, but that does not make them clean. As you stuff more and more dirty laundry into your bag, the job of cleaning it becomes bigger. Eventually, you will run out of clean clothes and have to face your dirty laundry.

When you stuff anger, you are running the risk of wasting energy without any benefits for yourself. Because a lot of your energy may be trapped in trying not to confront the anger, you will have less and less energy to enjoy the good times. When you stuff anger, you let it control you.

If you think that you don't see any of yourself in Sharon's tale, try looking a little closer. Even James, who could hardly be said to be shy about expressing anger, occasionally held it in instead. For example, one day after the incident in which he offended his "girlfriend," he again found himself in a confrontational situation. Normally, he would have struck out, but he still remembered what had happened the previous day, so he managed to hold the anger in. That would have been fine if James had been able to find a way to get rid of the anger in a nondestructive way. But, of course, he didn't. He "stewed" about it for one more day, and then took it out on an unsuspecting friend. You can guess the results.

▼

ASSIGNMENT 23

Directions:

1. In your notebook, write down any behaviors you have recognized in yourself that are the result of stuffing anger.

2. Do you know people (real people or fictional characters) who held their anger in? Who were they and how did they ultimately reveal their anger?

◄◄ UNIT 3 ►►
ESCALATING ANGER

The Meaning of Escalation

Escalation is another way in which people "handle" their anger. Escalation means making the anger bigger, or feeding the anger so that it will grow. How do people escalate anger? One of the ways is by having negative thoughts and engaging in negative self-talk. As we discussed before, in negative self-talk, a person makes negative statements to himself or herself that prolong or intensify a feeling. Remember the story about the aspiring cheerleader and her negative self-talk that resulted in making her feel angrier and angrier? Here is another example. The large numbers correspond with the anger intensities on an Anger Ruler.

"Cliff Jumping"

Cliff played shortstop on his high-school baseball team. Usually he was a starter, but one day his coach decided to start Robin because Cliff had not been really trying for the last two games. Cliff was not pleased. "Why is the coach letting Robin start?" he thought. "I've been hitting well and I haven't made a fielding error all week." Cliff was annoyed.

After three innings, the other team was leading 2 to 1. Robin had made an error that allowed a run to score. Cliff was wondering, "When is Coach going to put me in? It isn't right that our whole team should suffer because Robin isn't good enough. I wonder why Coach has it in for me."

In the fourth inning, Robin struck out with two players on base. Cliff was beginning to come unglued. "Man, this is terrible! Robin can't field and he can't hit. If I don't get into the game soon, we'll be so far behind them we won't have a chance. Coach doesn't even *look* at me." Cliff pounded a baseball into his glove over and over.

When his team took the field a few minutes later, Cliff started to get up and join them. Then he realized that he wasn't playing. His face reddened in embarrassment. "Now I look like a fool, too. It's all Coach's fault. He won't let me play just because he hates me. There's no other reason. I played hard all season and this is the thanks I get."

Robin made two good plays in the field, but by this time it didn't matter to Cliff. In just two more minutes, his anger had gotten away from him. He paced around the bench for a moment, then slammed the baseball into the dirt and headed for the exit. His coach asked Cliff where he was going. "If you're not going to play me, I quit!" Cliff yelled over his shoulder.

Cliff knew he had made a mistake, and he knew it was going to be difficult to undo the damage, but at that moment, he didn't care. He would care later, however. We will come back to Cliff's story at the end of this unit.

The acceleration of Cliff's anger is obvious, even without the numbers to make it visual. The mechanism for the acceleration is also obvious—Cliff's negative self-talk provided the energy. The cycle was set:

▼

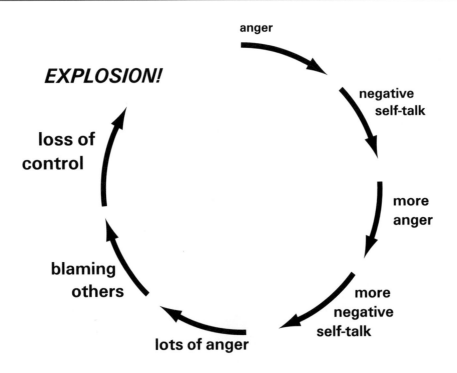

Figure 5. The anger self-talk cycle.

Denying Responsibility = Giving Up Control

Figure 5 illustrates an important point that we can find in Cliff's story. Cliff not only was angry because of circumstances (Robin's errors and strike-out), but he also started to blame the coach. By doing that, Cliff was refusing to take responsibility for what happened. He knew that he had been slacking off recently, especially during practice, but he didn't want to think about that.

By not accepting responsibility for what he did, Cliff made it almost impossible to "own" his anger. In this case, it is not likely that he will learn anything from the experience, and he will probably make the same mistake over and over again.

Every time you give up responsibility, you are giving up control. Cliff may have seen blaming the coach as an easy way out. It might have temporarily prevented him from feeling bad, but in the end, it would have created feelings of helplessness and frustration because he had given up control. How exactly did Cliff give up control? If Cliff had said to himself, "This is my fault; I haven't been trying hard enough," he would have been able to do something about the situation. He would have control over it. When he says, "It's all the coach's fault," there is nothing he can do—it is up to the coach and Cliff has no control.

▼

> **SUMMARY:** Give up responsibility—give up control. Take responsibility—take control.

ASSIGNMENT 24

Directions:

1. In your notebook, write down any behaviors you have recognized in yourself that are the result of escalating anger.

2. What AITs would work well if you were to find yourself escalating anger?

The End of Cliff's Story

Cliff didn't get thrown off the team, but the coach did make him apologize for his behavior in front of his teammates. Although this was hard for Cliff, it wouldn't be the last time an incident like this would occur. Cliff managed to finish the season, but it was so unpleasant that he didn't even try out for the team the next year. That was too bad, because at least two colleges had been thinking of offering Cliff a baseball scholarship.

◀◀ UNIT 4 ▶▶
DISPLACING ANGER

The Meaning of "Displacement"

Displacing anger means directing your response to angry feelings at someone or something that had nothing to do with your being angry. For example, a student upset with a teacher might be unable to express the anger directly to the teacher without risking serious consequences. So, the student displaces the anger and expresses it to a classmate who accidentally bumped into him or her.

Kicking the Dog?

Anger displacement can be seen as part of many other types of angry behavior. It is quite common. A very clear and amusing example is this true story told to me by a friend.

"When I was in graduate school," my friend began, "our department was very democratic. Most decisions were made by a faculty meeting at which graduate students were represented. I happened to be one of the graduate representives on the day that one of my classmates, Matt, appeared before the meeting to offer a suggestion.

"Matt told the department to buy a dog and keep it in the building. Whenever anyone got angry at something, he or she could call for the dog and kick it. He explained that it would be very inexpensive, since we could get the dog free at the animal shelter, and we wouldn't have to feed it since it would be kicked to death in a few days anyway."

Of course, Matt was only joking (a sick joke at that), but the story is still instructive. It appears that Matt was expressing a very real problem that he had not been able to solve. There are lots of frustrations in graduate school, and Matt undoubtedly had experienced his share. But when he got angry, Matt didn't know how to deal with his feelings in a positive way. Casting about for solutions, Matt came up with a strategy for displacing his anger. To his credit, Matt quickly realized that this was a losing strategy, and he turned it into a joke.

His question still remains: "How can I channel this anger so that I can get rid of it, or, better yet, so that I can turn it to my benefit?" I keep promising you the answer to this question, and I will keep that promise. But you and Matt will have to wait until the next chapter. In the meantime, it is important that you understand that displacing anger is a very poor strategy—it does little to relieve your anger and it often hurts other people, which ends up hurting you.

Other Examples of Displacing Anger

Let's take a quick look at some of the ways in which anger is displaced.

▸ John had a rather nasty boss who frequently made him angry. Because he couldn't express his anger at his boss without losing his job, when he came home, he found fault with anything his wife or children did.

▸ Harvey kicked furniture whenever his favorite team lost a game.

▸ Naomi cut off pieces of her hair when her latest boyfriend was seen with another girl.

These three examples show anger displaced to three different types of objects:

▸ John displaced his anger on other people.

▸ Harvey displaced his anger on inanimate objects.

▸ Naomi was mildly self-destructive, displacing her anger onto her own body.

ASSIGNMENT 25

Directions:

1. In Unit 3, you met Cliff, who got angry at his coach for not starting him in a baseball game. Cliff displaced his anger. What was the true source of Cliff's anger, and to whom or what did he displace it? Write your answer in your notebook. Then check the comment at the end of this assignment before going on to part 2.

2. Fill in the True Sources of Anger Frame that follows this assignment. Use your own experiences, things you have seen happen to your friends, or incidents from television, the movies, or books. For each, write down what happened in column 1. In column 2, fill in the true source

of the anger. In column 3, fill in the person or object to whom or to which the anger was displaced. You may not be able to fill in too many rows right now, so keep this Frame handy and enter more incidents as you notice them. If you are observant, you will find examples very frequently.

COMMENTS ON ASSIGNMENT 25

The displacement of anger is not always obvious. The source of Cliff's anger was *himself*. He knew he had not been trying hard enough during the past few games. But rather than admit his shortcoming, Cliff displaced his anger to his coach.

▼

TRUE SOURCES OF ANGER AND THEIR DISPLACED TARGETS

EVENT	TRUE SOURCE	DISPLACED TARGET

◄◄ UNIT 5 ►►
RESPONDING AGGRESSIVELY

Aggressive Responses May Start Early

Responding aggressively to angry feelings refers to a physical response. You have come to know that James responded aggressively to anger in many situations. This behavior actually started when he was very young. His mother reported that as a young child, James often hit and kicked adults and other children. He was rarely disciplined for these displays because his father thought it was "manly." James even had an uncle who would taunt him until James started punching, and would then hold him at arm's length.

We will never know to what extent these incidents contributed to James' aggressive behaviors, but we do know that by the time he was 10, he could hit hard enough that no one considered it funny anymore. He also liked to punch walls, kick toys, and throw pencils at people. By the time he entered his teens, James' behavior was getting him into trouble, and finally it landed him in a juvenile institution.

Why did James use aggression as a means of venting his anger? Actually, a lot of people do. One of the reasons is that some people report feeling better immediately after responding aggressively. The immediate release of pent-up energy is a relief. Unfortunately, the good feeling seldom lasts very long.

The Problem with Aggression

Aggression creates its own set of problems. For one thing, it often hurts other people. Those other people frequently respond to being hurt, and that response can be very serious. How many times have you heard of someone being injured or even killed by a person responding to an initial act of anger?

It recently happened in the city where I live. A young man driving his car to work on the freeway got angry at another motorist who cut into his lane right in front of him. After slamming on his brakes to avoid an accident, our unfortunate driver made an obscene gesture in the direction of the other car. Suddenly, a window of the other car was rolled down, a gun was pointed and fired, and a 22-year-old who had vented his anger with an obscene gesture died.

Aggression Hurts the Aggressor, Too

In addition to hurting other people, aggressive responses can hurt *you*. One way in which this happens is through guilty feelings. For example, if a boy hits his friend in anger, he may feel guilty for hurting him. Guilt is a very difficult feeling to deal with, so the boy may try to feel better by using negative self-talk to explain his behavior. And we know what happens next.

"I hit him because he was being a jerk," the boy might say to himself. "He knew I was getting angry and didn't back off." Or: "He's not a good friend and deserves what he got." This kind of self-talk denies responsibility and generates more anger. In the process of denying responsibility, you may end up losing a valuable friendship. Ask James: he knows all about it.

Other Ways to Feel Good

Because the immediate release of energy through aggression might feel good temporarily, aggression may be difficult to give up unless you find something that feels just as good, such as relaxation or enjoyable activities that require energy. Some people need a physical outlet for their anger, but it does not have to be a destructive one. There are many physical things that people can do when they are angry that do not involve hurting others.

Among physical activities that release energy are running; playing a sport, such as basketball (you may want to shoot hoops by yourself if you are very angry); one-person racketball; and swimming. These activities both are fun and use up a lot of energy. You can think of other physical activities that help release energy—in fact, let's make an assignment out of it.

ASSIGNMENT 26

Directions:

1. On a sheet of paper in your notebook, list at least five physical activities that you enjoy.

2. Next to each one, place a star if you feel that this activity would be useful in releasing anger without hurting other people.

COMMENTS ON ASSIGNMENT 26

Healthy physical activity does not have to be aggressive activity. For example, I do not recommend boxing as a way to release angry energy because boxing is an aggressive sport that may actually reinforce the aggressive behavior instead of releasing energy. Boxing, ice hockey, and other aggressive physical sports have their place, but they are not a good idea for a person with an anger problem.

To relieve angry tension, use physical activities that make you feel calm and relaxed, but that are not aggressive in nature.

◄◄ UNIT 6 ►►
USING DRUGS OR ALCOHOL

Drugs and Alcohol

Using drugs or alcohol to calm down is another way in which some people deal with anger. But the results of dealing with anger in this way are similar to the results of responding aggressively. Using drugs or alcohol may provide immediate relief from an uncomfortable feeling, but it does not solve the problem that triggered the angry response.

Whenever Stuart had a bad day at work, he would stop at a bar on his way home. After a few beers, Stuart would tell his tales of woe to the bartender or anyone else unlucky enough to be near enough to hear. He could usually count on a few sympathetic words, especially from the bartender, whom Stuart always tipped well. When he got home, his wife would usually be displeased with him. Apparently, her idea of a good husband was not one who came home late, drunk, and broke. Since Stuart's wife was one of those persons who respond to anger with aggression, Stuart often ended up with a few bruises to go along with his hangover.

Stuart Knows He Is Solving Nothing, But ...

If you asked Stuart why he continued behaviors that were clearly causing him problems, he would tell you that the drinking helped him to calm down. He would even begin to feel good about his work. By the time he had downed three or four, his anger would be gone. It was worth his wife's rage, the hangover, and being broke just to relieve the angry energy that had built up within him.

Stuart knew that when he woke up in the morning and had to face going to work again, he would have *solved nothing*. The easy way to feel good had deprived Stuart of the chance to deal with the problem that caused the anger.

Stuart was not a fool—he understood all of this. But he had never learned any other way to vent his anger, so when it got bad enough, he always turned to alcohol.

Just as responding aggressively leaves a path of destruction along its way, so does using drugs or alcohol. Drugs and alcohol create a new set of problems that will contribute to continued bad feelings and anger. The anger cycle eventually worsens. Running away from problems does not make the problems disappear.

> **SUMMARY:** People who use drugs or alcohol often resent anyone telling them they should stop. Regardless of how you may feel about these substances in general, please believe this. Using drugs or alcohol to relieve anger causes many, many more problems than it solves.

Looking Ahead

This completes our survey of five types of angry behaviors that do not work. If you have seen some of yourself in any of these, you should try to avoid them. The next chapter will reveal a new set of behaviors that express anger effectively and use its power to get you what you want and need.

CHAPTER 5

▼

THE EFFECTIVE USE OF ANGER

◄◄ **UNIT 1** ►►

COMMUNICATING YOUR ANGER

A Decision Point

So far you have learned to recognize your anger, and you have mastered some techniques to bring it under control. These skills allow you to avoid the embarrassing and dangerous incidents that result from runaway anger. You can do these things right now, and, as you continue to practice, you will be able to do them better and more often.

Despite these gains, you may feel that you have been left halfway through a long journey. You have been climbing a high mountain and have finally reached a flat area where you can pause and catch your breath. The higher parts of the mountain are covered with clouds, and you can't really see where the path leads. It might be tempting to stop here and say "good enough." After all, you have accomplished a great deal, the view is beautiful even here, and the rest of the route up is very uncertain.

Fortunately, you have two guides—your counselor and this workbook. And these guides are telling you to press onward. The path is known, and it is a good one. The climb is not nearly so steep from now on, and the view from the top of the mountain is well worth the effort.

A Glimpse of Beyond

The next part of the trail leads you to Assertiveness Ridge, where the astonishing power of a magic word will be revealed. Then the trail turns to the right, climbs a small rise, and opens onto a sparkling vista called Point of View. From there, you will be able to see any event from all sides, an ability that will give you remarkable power to control any situation.

Does this sound overstated to you? Can this workbook possibly deliver on my promises? You'll never know if you don't continue your journey with mind opened wide and a resolve to reach the top.

Inside or Outside?

When you feel anger, you can do one of two things with it: you can keep it inside yourself or you can let it out. Sharon's problem was that she kept anger inside; because she could not express it, she was unable to get any relief until her frustrations had grown to the breaking point. Since keeping anger inside you doesn't work very well, the only thing left is to let it out.

Letting anger out means expressing it. James expressed his anger physically, and that got him into trouble. Then how should you express your anger? To answer that question, let's look at a short example.

Richard is your friend, but today you are angry at him. Richard had two tickets to a rock concert. Instead of asking you to go with him, he asked his dorky kid brother! What should you do? Pick the best of these choices.

a. Nothing.
b. Tell Richard that he's a jerk.
c. Tell Richard's kid brother that he's a dork.
d. Ask Richard why he didn't offer you the ticket.
e. Beat up Richard's kid brother.

If you picked the first option (a), you have just stuffed your anger, which we have seen is not an effective solution. The other solutions all involve expressing your anger, which is good. But if you picked the last choice (e), you have James' problem—violence rarely resolves a situation in a satisfactory manner. The remaining choices (b, c, and d) involve expressing your anger in words; this is the approach that usually works. So which of the three is the best?

Communication

All three remaining choices have you telling someone about your anger. They are all examples of *communication*. Communicating your anger is desirable. Before going further, however, here is something for you to think about: was choice (e), beating up Richard's brother, also a form of communication? Answer this question for yourself before reading the next paragraph.

Beating up Richard's brother is, indeed, a kind of communication. But it is a very incomplete one. Communication means the sharing of an idea with another person. After being beaten to a pulp, Richard's brother will know that you are angry, but he won't know with whom you are angry or what you are angry about. Therefore, even if he wanted to do something to help you resolve your anger, he would have no idea of what to do. Clearly, this is a poor form of communication—it's like a radio station with so much static that you can barely understand any words.

Communication to the Proper Person

Let's get back to choices (b), (c), and (d). All three are communication. But choices (b) and (d) express your anger to Richard, who is the cause of the anger. This makes sense. Choice (c) expresses your anger to Richard's kid brother, who is not the one who contributed to your anger. This is unfair. It also won't do you any good.

That leaves choices (b) and (d). Both are communication to the proper person, Richard. But one choice is much better than the other.

Communicating What You Are Trying to Communicate

What exactly are you trying to tell Richard? First, you want to let him know that you are angry with him. Second, you want to find out if Richard had a good reason for giving the ticket to his brother. Third, if he didn't have a compelling reason to do so, you want to make sure that the next time this situation occurs, you get a chance at the ticket.

Choice (b)—telling Richard that he's a jerk—accomplishes only the first of these three goals. Choice (d) accomplishes them all, which is why it is the best choice.

It Really Is Not That Easy

It might seem as though we have completed the goal for the entire chapter. After all, you already knew how to recognize your anger. You knew how to use AITs to interrupt the anger cycle and regain control. And now you have learned that the next step is to communicate your anger to the person responsible for it.

Of course, it's really not that easy. In fact, expressing anger when you have not learned how to do it can be very difficult. This is especially true when the anger is very intense and you feel overwhelmed. The remainder of this chapter will help you build the skills that allow you to communicate your anger powerfully and effectively, even under the most trying conditions.

◀◀ UNIT 2 ▶▶
AN APOLOGY—IS IT ENOUGH?

Clara and Joe Apologize

When you get angry because someone said something that hurt your feelings, an apology might be enough. In other cases, it is necessary to change a situation in order to solve the problem. For example, Joe accidentally hits you with his elbow when he turns around without looking. "Sorry," he says. You know it was an accident; Joe is unlikely to hit you again that way. The apology is enough to satisfy you.

Another example: Clara is always gossiping. You hear her telling one of your friends something untrue about you. You confront her with her lie and she apologizes. Is this apology enough? I don't think it is. First, Clara has not undone the damage she did; somehow she has to admit the lie to your friend. Second, Clara will probably do something like this again.

Sometimes an apology is enough; sometimes it isn't. Let's look at another situation that's not quite so simple.

Sharon Gets a Better Job

Sharon's breaking up with Clark might have been a relief, but it also caused a lot of problems. One of them was money. In order to continue being a part-time graduate student, Sharon had to have a better-paying job. Since she was educated, had a neat appearance, and expressed herself well in job interviews, she soon found one.

In her new job as a design assistant at a jewelry store, Sharon helped the jewelry designers make custom rings, necklaces, and earrings. It was challenging and fun, and it paid well.

Within a week of taking the job, Sharon noticed that daily her boss would have new little tasks for her, some of which she really disliked. She felt that since she was hired as a design assistant, taking out the garbage was not part of the job. Since Sharon was still not very good at expressing her anger, she just did the tasks and said nothing.

One day, she told us about it: "It looks like Harry, my boss, changes my job description without taking my feelings into account. It started to annoy me last week, and it keeps happening. But I keep plugging along, because I really like the rest of the job and the people I work with are great."

The next time we met, things had become worse. Sharon told us that on the previous day, her boss had asked her to put a new cartridge in the laser printer. "I had no idea how to do it," she said. "But I found the instruction book next to the machine. Of course, it didn't tell me where to find the new cartridges, but I finally tracked them down in a storage cabinet. I was annoyed at my boss for giving me yet another job. But it didn't look too difficult. So I followed the instructions step by step.

"I opened the printer, pulled out the old cartridge, and tore the tape off the new one. Inside was the toner, which is a fine, black powder. I tried to be very careful, but it was hard to fit the new cartridge into the printer, and I ended up getting some of the toner on my brand-new shirt. In case you want to know, you can't get toner off of a silk shirt by brushing it, and you certainly don't put water on it.

"I was really starting to get angry. It was Harry's fault for asking me to do something I didn't know how to do. My shirt was dirty. I didn't know if that stuff would ever come off, and worse yet, I had a date right after work." Sharon blushed a little here; it was the first we had heard about her going out after splitting up with Clark. "Anyway," she went on, "going home would make me late to meet my date, and I didn't want to do that because I was a half hour late the last time.

"I wanted to go into my boss' office and tell him he was a jerk. I wished I could just let him have it. Wouldn't you know, Harry walks by at just that time. He looks at my dirty shirt, and then looks at the toner cartridge. Then he shows me how to put it in and says he's sorry that my shirt got dirty."

ASSIGNMENT 27

Directions:

1. When Sharon brought this incident up in her next therapy session, she realized that the apology was not enough to satisfy her. In your notebook, write down the reasons why the apology probably seemed insufficient to Sharon.

▼

COMMENTS ON ASSIGNMENT 27

There are really two problems with Harry's response to Sharon's situation. First, the wrong has not been set right. Sharon has a dirty shirt that, at the very least, will cost her several dollars to clean. Furthermore, she is going to have to spend extra time to get the shirt clean. Second, there is a bigger problem here—Sharon does not feel that she was hired to do some of the tasks that are being assigned to her. Harry probably doesn't even know about that problem.

"I guess Harry noticed that I was still upset," Sharon went on. "He told me he would pay to have the shirt cleaned. I thought that was nice of him, so I just let the rest of it go, but I was still mad. I even snuck off of work 10 minutes early to beat some of the traffic, so I wouldn't be too late for my date."

We told Sharon that she was being a wimp (well, maybe we didn't use the word "wimp"). "Listen," I told her, "having Harry pay for the dry cleaning may have made you feel a little bit better at the time. But is your problem solved? Next time your boss comes up with a new dumb job for you, will you get angry all over again?"

"That's exactly what I concluded in my last session," Sharon admitted. "The basic problem still remained. But what else could I have said?"

ASSIGNMENT 28

Directions:

1. In your notebook, write down what you think Sharon should have said to her boss. Then read it aloud, pretending that Harry is standing in front of you. If it doesn't sound right, revise it until you are pleased with your response. Do not read the rest of this assignment until you have completed this part.

2. For each of the following possible responses, write down in your notebook whether you feel the response was good or it could be improved. If you think it could be improved, write down what was wrong with it and/or how it could be made better.

    a. "Harry, you make me so angry. Why do you give me these dumb jobs? Just let me do the work you hired me for!"

    b. "You're darn right you'll pay for the dry cleaning. And I'm also taking off a half hour early to go home to change."

    c. "I'm a little bit upset by this and I'd like to leave early so I can change my shirt before my appointment. But what really is bothering me is that I don't think I was hired to change toner cartridges and take out garbage."

3. Read the comment on this assignment before doing part 4.

4. Examine the response you wrote down in part 1 of this assignment. Does it communicate the five points listed in the comments on Assignment 28? If it doesn't, revise your response to include the missing points.

COMMENTS ON ASSIGNMENT 28

Here are some thoughts on part 2 of the assignment. Sharon should communicate at least these points to Harry.

1. That she is angry.
2. The immediate cause of her anger (her dirty shirt).
3. What she wants to have done about the dirty shirt.
4. The basic cause of her anger (being given lots of odd jobs).
5. What she wants to do about the odd jobs.

Now let's take a look at how well the following three responses communicate these five points.

a. 1—yes. 2—no. 3—no. 4—yes. 5—partly, but Harry is not being given a chance to present his viewpoint. Sharon is not leaving the door open to sharing these tasks with the other people in the office.

b. 1—yes (by her tone and strong language). 2—yes (not actually said, but clear from the dry-cleaning and time-off statements). 3—yes. 4—no. 5—no.

c. 1—yes. 2—yes. 3—yes. 4—yes. 5—no. This is a very good response, lacking only one more sentence, such as, "Let's talk tomorrow morning about exactly what my duties should be."

SUMMARY: Two things that must be communicated are what's bothering you and what you want to do about it.

The Magic Word

There is a "magic" word in the best of three sample responses in Assignment 28. Can you spot it?

Take another look at your response and the three sample responses. For each sentence in each response, see if an "I" word ("I," "me," "my") is used before a "you" word ("you," "your," "Harry"). Notice that in the best sample response (c), both sentences have "I" words first.

Effectively communicating anger starts with an assertive "I" statement. Why an "I" statement? By saying "I" instead of "you," you are letting the other person know that you are accepting responsibility for your feelings, and that you are communicating that it is important to change the situation. This is a way of being assertive and responsible.

The magic word turns out to be one letter long!

The Other Magic Word

The other magic word is not one that you speak. Instead, it is something that you can be—assertive. Being *assertive* means recognizing what you need and standing up for yourself so that you can get it. "Harry, you skunk, I'm leaving early to go change my shirt. And you are going to stop dumping all of these stupid little jobs on me. Get it?" seems to meet this definition. It certainly recognizes what you need and you would definitely be standing up for yourself. But this statement is not assertive. It goes too far. Instead of being assertive, it is *aggressive*.

Being assertive also requires that you take into account other people's rights and needs. It is a way in which you can be considerate and *still* get what you want. You might think: "How can this be done? Do I have to say 'Harry, please don't be angry, but I really would appreciate it if you would let me take a few minutes off to go home and change my shirt, if that wouldn't be any problem to you?'" Of course not—that is not assertive either. But often the difference between assertiveness and aggressiveness is not obvious. So we are going to take a couple of entire units to learn how to respond assertively to anger.

◀◀ **UNIT 3** ▶▶
OPTIONS

Three Different Reactions

In this unit, we are going to look at how three different people would behave in a common situation. We will call them X, Y, and Z. For this unit, they all will be male, but there are plenty of females with the same personalities.

X = Aggressive

X is an aggressive person. He always "takes care of himself" and gets what he wants, no matter who gets hurt in the process. On a grade-school food line, X is the boy who switches his small piece of pie for your large one. Even his high-school football coach has to tell him to "cool it." X is the kind who shoots first and asks questions later (if he asks questions at all).

Y = Passive

Y appears to be the opposite of X. He is passive. You would probably say that he lets people walk all over him, but he wouldn't describe himself that way. He would just say that he doesn't like to fight. Y does not take care of his own needs. If a store clerk gives him too little change, Y will take what was offered. You might think it would be perfectly safe to treat Y anyway you wanted to, and you would be right—about 99 percent of the time. The exception occurs when Y's anger and frustration build up to the breaking point. When this happens, watch out!

Z = Assertive

There must be a happy medium between X and Y. That would be Z. Z takes care of himself, but he goes beyond that. He recognizes that other people have feelings, thoughts, and basic rights. He is usually able to get what he wants without antagonizing others. Z recognizes his needs, but weighs them against other people's needs and rights. His is a balanced way of getting needs met. It is a much healthier way to share the world, and does not jeopardize his relationships with others.

A Common Situation

How would you react in a common situation like this one? Imagine that you are standing in line at the express lane at a grocery store. Someone cuts in front of you. How do you respond? Take a moment to think about this before reading further.

As you tried to decide how to respond to this situation, you may have had some questions. For example:

1. Did the person who cut in do so on purpose, or did he or she just not notice you?
2. Are you in a hurry?
3. Does the person look normal and stable, or is the person a large violent-looking man?

Let's see how X, Y, and Z would react to this situation.

X Reacts

X really doesn't care about the answers to questions 1, 2, and 3. No matter what the details, X reacts aggressively. He is not going to let anyone push him around, and that's all there is to it. So X does something like one of these.

- Pushes the person out of the way and steps back in front of him or her.
- Says, "Hey, I was here first, so get behind me!"
- Yells to the cashier, "Will you tell this jerk to go to the end of the line?"

What are the consequences of this likely to be? In most cases, X ends up going ahead of the person who cut in. He definitely has not made any friends. This can cost him. For example, if the cashier thinks a package may leak a little, he or she will pack it in an extra bag. However, cashiers are people too, and when annoyed, they react. If X has a leaky package of fish, the cashier might just pack it in with the rest of the groceries. I hope X likes his lettuce soaked in fish juice.

Y Reacts

Y is like X in one way—he doesn't care about the answers to questions 1, 2, and 3 either. No matter what, Y is not going to do anything. In fact, this is not a problem to Y at all—he doesn't even think about doing anything.

What are the consequences for Y? He will not antagonize anyone; the cashier will double-bag his fish. In most cases, nothing really bad happens to Y—unless, that is, he is already late for a date. You can complete that scenario for yourself.

Z Reacts

Z is an assertive person. He will consider his needs and the needs of the person who cut in line in front of him. The answers to questions 1, 2, and 3 are important to Z. For example, if Z is not in a hurry and he doesn't think the person cutting in noticed him, Z will not do anything. He has no need to. Being fifth in line instead of fourth will not hurt him significantly, and he sees no need to make another person feel bad.

If Z were in a hurry, very likely he would do something to assure that his needs were met. If the person who cut in appeared to be a reasonable individual, Z would probably decide to ask him or her to step back in line. He would express this with an "I" statement (we will practice these statements later in this chapter).

On the other hand, if the person who cut in is not likely to be receptive to an assertive approach (he is big, he looks mean, he hasn't shaved in two days, his demeanor is rude, and he wears an angry scowl), Z has to consider his response. By asking him to give Z his place back in the line, Z might start a bigger hassle than the gain would be worth. Z might even end up needing minor surgery. The result might be to make Z even later than if he had said nothing. Remember, the purpose of being assertive is to get your needs met, and right now being on time is what Z needs to do. In such a situation, an assertive person chooses the option that is most likely to result in being on time.

If the person who cut in appeared to do so intentionally, Z might take some action even if he were not in a hurry. In this case, what Z would be trying to accomplish is saving time. Since this is not very important, Z would not take much risk to obtain it. However, if the person ahead of him appears to be friendly, Z might do something like clearing his throat. The person who cut in would probably notice, realize that he or she has been caught, and beat an embarrassed retreat to the back of the line.

Comparing the Reactions

Did you notice that the section about Z's response is much longer than the sections for X and Y? There is a good reason for this. Aggressive and passive people just do not have many choices! There isn't much to say for them. An assertive person, with many more options among which to choose, is much more likely to find one that "works."

▼

◀◀ UNIT 4 ▶▶
THE AGGRESSIVE–ASSERTIVE–PASSIVE CONTINUUM

A Balancing Act

There is no sharp line dividing aggressive behavior from assertive, or assertive behavior from passive. They merge gradually into one another, forming a continuum, as illustrated in Figure 6.

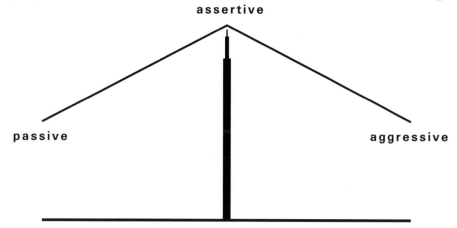

Figure 6. Assertive behavior is a balance between passive and aggressive behavior.

ASSIGNMENT 29

Directions:

1. Listed below are five groups, each containing three characteristics. In each group, one characteristic is typical of the passive person, one is typical of the assertive person, and one is typical of the aggressive person. Next to each put a "P" for passive, "A" for aggressive or "+" for assertive.

_____ Allows others to take advantage and violate his or her rights.

_____ Takes advantage of others and violates their rights.

_____ Stands up for his or her rights while respecting the rights of others.

_____ Uses others to attempt to meet his or her own needs and goals.

_____ Knows how to get needs met while being considerate of others.

_____ Does not know how to get needs met; does not achieve goals.

_____ Has good self-esteem and is realistic about his or her capabilities.

_____ Is hostile, defensive; puts others down; appears confident, but isn't.

_____ Has poor self-esteem; feels unfulfilled, helpless, frustrated, anxious.

_____ Is socially inept, withdrawn, unsure, inhibited.

_____ Is socially adept, with good social and emotional skills.

_____ Has social problems owing to explosive unpredictable behavior.

_____ Makes own choices; also tries to make others' decisions for them.

_____ Makes own choices and takes responsibility for them.

_____ Gives up the power to make choices and the responsibility.

COMMENTS ON ASSIGNMENT 29

The answers are:

Group 1: P, A, +

Group 2: A, +, P

Group 3: +, A, P

Group 4: P, +, A

Group 5: A, +, P

Who Is Happy Around Here?

By now, you probably have come to the conclusion that you want to be an assertive person. You know that the passive person is likely to be unhappy. He or she does not have an opportunity to have his or her needs met, because he or she is not likely to express those needs. The passive person allows things to happen, and takes a helpless approach to life.

The aggressive person is also likely to be unhappy. Whereas he or she attempts to get needs met by being aggressive, his or her behavior is likely to cause many social problems.

The assertive person is at the happy medium, where needs are met but not at the expense of others. When you are assertive, you are respecting your rights, as well as the other person's rights. You can be happy while allowing others the same opportunity. Assertive individuals have a better chance of getting their needs met, because they express what they need in a way that increases their chances of getting it.

ASSIGNMENT 30

Directions:

1. The Assertiveness Table following this assignment contains two columns. In the first is a code indicating various types of personalities. PPP means very passive, PP is somewhat passive, P is slightly passive, AAA is very aggressive, AA is somewhat aggressive, and A is slightly aggressive. The + in the middle is for balanced, assertive personalities.

For each of the following people, decide where they belong on this continuum and write the person's name in the second column next to the proper code:

X

Y

Z

James

Sharon

yourself

2. Add other people to the table. Select them from among your relatives and friends. You may also use television or movie characters, people in the news, or even animals. Try to fill in at least two names for each code. For fun, add your counselor to the table!

ASSERTIVENESS TABLE

	PEOPLE
PPP	
PP	
P	
+	
A	
AA	
AAA	

◄◄ UNIT 5 ►►
REVISITING THE MAGIC WORD

In a previous unit, the magic word "I" was revealed. In this unit, you will learn the proper way to use this magic word in an assertive manner.

"I" Versus "You"

Communicating anger in an assertive manner takes a lot of practice. Sometimes it is difficult to accept responsibility for feelings, especially when you are very angry, and when you think that others contributed to your anger. But the truth is that *you* hold the power of anger, and *you* can use it in many ways.

Being assertive requires new communication skills that demonstrate respect for yourself and for other people. "I" statements, as opposed to "You" statements, are essential in communicating anger appropriately. Consider these two ways of expressing an angry sentiment:

A. "You're really making me angry and you're going to regret it!"

B. "I'm very angry at what you did and I think that at least I should get an apology."

The (A) sentence is a "You" statement. Put yourself in the other person's place. How would he or she interpret what you said? I think it would be something like this.

"What do you know? I have the power to make him angry—so angry, in fact, that he lost control of himself. What should I do now? I don't really want to hurt him, but I don't know what he expects of me. If I apologize, he might think that makes me weak and then decide to do something to 'make me regret it.' I think it would be better for me to remain in control of the situation, so I'll just walk away."

This is not exactly what the angry person hoped to communicate, but what can you expect from statements that give up responsibility and control to the other person ("You")? The (A) sentence is a threat and it gives the initiative to the other person. Most people react to threats either defensively or aggressively. In either case, you can't get much out of them.

The (B) sentence is an "I" statement. It takes responsibility for being angry, lets the other person know it, and tells him or her what you want to have done. How would the other person react? Perhaps it would be like this.

"Apparently he got angry at me for what I did. I really don't want to make him angry. He says I should apologize, and that seems fair. Maybe I should even go a bit further. What can I do to make him feel better?"

The Two Parts of an Assertive Statement

An assertive statement to communicate anger needs to contain two thoughts:
- That you are angry and why you are angry.
- What you want the other person to do about it.

If you express yourself using "I" sentences and make sure you include the above two points, you almost surely will have made an assertive response to anger.

A simple form of such a statement is: "I feel angry because _____. I want you to _____." Every case is different, however, and so the words you use will also differ. Try to follow these three simple rules.
- Use "I" statements.
- Express why you are angry and what you want done about it.
- Avoid name calling.

ASSIGNMENT 31

Directions:

1. Convert each of these "You" statements into an "I" statement.

   a. "You can't get away with hitting me. If you do it again, you'll be sorry."

   _____

   _____

   b. "Can't you understand that you are just being stupid when you gossip? You should be ashamed to show your face among my friends."

   _____

   _____

2. Which of the three rules is violated in each of the above examples? Did you follow these rules in your "I" statements?

3. Take a situation from your life or one you have seen on television or in the movies. Imagine that it happened to you. Stand in front of a mirror and make an assertive statement about your anger. Do it out loud. What would the other person's response to your statement probably have been? It you don't like that response, try modifying your statement until you think you would get a response you do like. You can also rehearse this in front of your counselor.

"I" Statements When You Are Not Angry

The magic "I" word works in many situations, including those in which you are not angry. "I" statements let the other person know that you are in control. They may feel awkward or strange at first, so it is important to practice them when you are not angry. In this way, they will become natural to you, so that you will use them easily to express your anger.

When is a good time to use "I" statements? Actually, they work well in almost any situation when you want another person to act in a certain way. For example, "I would appreciate faster service" is better than "Do you have to be so slow?" For the next few days, make a conscious effort to use "I" statements. Every time you do, score one point for yourself. See if you can get up to 10 points each day.

"I" Statements to Yourself

You can combine "I" statements with some of the AITs that you learned. For example, when you start to get angry, take a deep breath and say to yourself, "I am getting angry." Continue taking deep breaths as you sort out in your mind why you are angry, and what you want done about it. If negative thoughts pop up, such as, "She makes me so angry," stop these thoughts, and replace them with "I" statements, such as, "I am very angry because…" Your positive self-talk will be extremely effective. In addition, this paves the way for your next step (in the next chapter): once you know what you want done, you can use problem solving to determine how to get it!

ASSIGNMENT 32

Directions:

1. This is not an assignment you can do right now, but it is very important in getting you into the habit of making assertive responses to anger.

For the next week, try very hard to follow the examples of this unit. Make assertive responses to every angry situation—even those when you only become mildly angry. Most important, record these experiences in your anger journal. If you didn't respond the way you would have liked to respond, write that down too. Nobody is perfect.

2. At the end of the week, read your journal entries. Do you think it got easier to make assertive responses as the week went by?

(By the way, you should use your anger journal to record angry episodes, no matter what the outcome, as long as you are using this workbook.)

◄◄ UNIT 6 ►►
OTHER TYPES OF ANGER

Anger at a System

In Chapter 2, I described the peace demonstrators of the early 1970s. People gathered in large numbers to protest the Vietnam war. They were angry, but their anger was, for the most part, not focused on a single person. Of course, there were speeches against the President, various members of Congress, the Secretary of Defense, and anybody else who didn't agree with them, but the anger was really against a political system that started a war.

Suppose you were one of those protestors and that you had to make a statement about your anger. Since you had been reading this workbook, you wanted your statement to be an "I" statement, and you wanted it to explain why you were angry and what you wanted done about it. You might start off: "I'm angry because my country is involved in an unjust war. I want you...." That's when it gets hard.

You could say: "I want the war to stop." The problem with that is that it sounds like a wish. ("Wouldn't it be nice if the war ended?") You really want some action. Since systems do not take action unless people within them do something, you might say: "I want the President to stop the war." You might even be able to do something to influence the President, such as starting a letter-writing campaign. Then you realize that the President, by himself, *cannot* stop the war.

Next, you might say: "I want Congress to cut off all funding for the war, so then it will have to stop." But you know that "Congress" is made up of 535 people, a majority of whom would have to vote for a cutoff of funds. It seems hopeless that you could write enough letters to 535 people to do any good.

Then you begin to understand something. Your being at the peace rally *is* your "I" statement of anger. By being there, you are telling everyone in the system that you are angry and that you want the war stopped. You are telling each one of them individually that you want him or her to do what he or she can to stop the war. You *are* expressing your anger, and you are doing it in an assertive way.

Sometimes you cannot, by yourself, do anything about a situation that is making you angry. Perhaps by banding together with others, you can make a difference. In some cases, even that will not help. But there is always something you can do to express your anger assertively, even if it is only writing a letter that you know will not change the situation. Should you write that letter? Of course, you should. By expressing the anger, you will help to relieve it. In addition, writing that letter will *focus* your anger on the persons or systems that caused it. This will let the rest of us off the hook; you won't mistakenly direct your anger and frustration at us!

▼

SUMMARY: Expressing anger not only can get you what you want, but it can also make you feel better about yourself.

When You Really, Really Can't Do Anything!

There are some times when there is absolutely nothing you or anyone else can do about your anger. Suppose that for weeks you have been looking forward to going to a dance. You finally got that dreamy girl down the block to agree to go out with you. You have spent all of your money to rent a tuxedo and a limousine and to buy an expensive corsage for your date. The day before the dance you get the measles. You have no idea how you could have caught them, but there is no way you are going to get to that dance.

You are angry, but not at a specific person, or even at a system. You are angry at fate—at your bad luck. "I'm really angry that I got the measles," you think to yourself, "and I want . . ." It is pretty tough to finish that sentence with anything meaningful.

What do you do with that type of anger? Take a minute to think of your answer before you go any further.

This is really an exercise in problem solving (we'll get to that later in the workbook). As far as your anger goes, the important thing is to realize that no one is responsible for it. Therefore, you should be careful not to take out your frustrations on innocent bystanders. Being nasty to your mother will not speed your recovery by even one second. Another thing you have to recognize in this situation is that there is nothing you can, or even need to, do about this anger. Figuring out its cause (which was easy enough) is all that is needed. Do whatever AIT works best for you, calm down, and let your anger go. Positive self-talk will help.

Actually, there are some things you can do about this mess. First, you can try to get the money back that you laid out for the tuxedo and limousine rentals. Second, you can send the corsage to your date; that would be a nice gesture. Then you can call her to apologize; maybe she'll go out with you after you recover. Your self-talk can be very positive: "After all, there will be other dances. If I send her the corsage, I can ask if she'll go out with me next week. That would be even better. At the dance, we would be with lots of other people, but if she goes to a movie with me, I'll get to know her better. This might work out after all."

SUMMARY: It is absolutely amazing what positive thinking can accomplish!

▼

Old Anger

There is another kind of anger that may be difficult to deal with—old anger. Some people stay angry at things that happened a long time ago. This is particularly likely to happen if they have not dealt with the anger. The strategies that deal with new anger also work for old anger. But first it is necessary to recognize that it is old anger that is causing feelings and behaviors in the present.

James had progressed so far that he was scheduled to be released from the institution in just a few days. When he first found out about it, he was overjoyed. By our last session, however, he had become subdued. When I asked him how he felt about going home, he just said, "Okay." Clearly, something was bothering him.

We talked for almost an hour before James himself discovered the source of his feelings.

"I guess I'm still a little angry about my father," James began. I knew that James' father had deserted his family when James was very young, and that James had never known him. "All my life, it's been tough on Mom and tough on us kids. There has never been enough money. Mom wore herself out working and trying to raise us. We're doing okay now, but I can't help thinking how much better it could have been." Here James paused. I could see the anger in his eyes. He used what he had been learning to control it, but it was a battle. His voice quivered in tension as he continued.

"There's just nothing I can do about it. He's gone. No one knows where he is. He's never coming back." James' voice rose and he jumped to his feet. I won't record the names he called his father; you can make up a string of your own. Finally, he calmed down and sat back down in his chair. "I guess I really blew it now," he said.

James was ashamed that he had lost control. He had been very proud of controlling his anger and being assertive; there had not been one incident at the institution in over two months. What had happened this time?

I helped James understand that he had come across the hardest type of anger with which he would have to deal—old anger. He had been angry at his father for his entire life, and he had been unable to do anything about it. While at the institution, he had been able to put this anger away in the back of his mind. But going home and seeing his family again would bring it all back.

What should James do about this source of anger? Answer this question to yourself before reading on.

The same skills that James used to control his other types of anger will work with old anger. He can use his AITs to bring his anger under control. Then positive self-talk will help: "We're getting by just fine without him. I'm probably a stronger person for it. Mom's happy now, and we're much closer than my friends' families are." The important thing for James was to recognize the source of his anger, and to understand that there was nothing he could or needed to do to change the circumstances.

With this understanding, James went home.

▼

◄◄ UNIT 7 ►►
INTERPRETING EVENTS

This chapter has taken you a long way toward using anger effectively. You have learned about assertive behavior—getting your needs met, while also taking other people's needs and feelings into account. You have learned a skill (the "I" statement) to help you react assertively to angry situations. And you have learned that an effective assertive response usually addresses the issues of why you are angry and what you want done about it.

It is important that you practice what you have learned in this chapter, even if it means taking a few days off from this workbook. This unit is one that you can do while you are perfecting your assertiveness skills.

Under Attack

It is difficult to be assertive when you feel that you are under attack. But just because you *feel* you are under attack doesn't mean that you really are. In this unit, you will see how the way you interpret events may add to your problems with managing your anger by causing you to feel attacked when actually you are not.

Different People See Things Differently

You know that different people see things differently. For example, suppose you saw a movie with a friend. Have you noticed how you and your friend might describe the same movie very differently? Your friend might talk about a "great" chase scene, while you hardly remember it. You might have particularly liked the acting of one of the stars; your friend may have hated it. Yet it was the same movie that you both watched.

We "see" things differently because we give different meanings to what appear to be the same events. The external world (the world outside of you) may be the same, but the internal world (the world inside of you) is as unique as each person. Your internal world is made up of who you are physically and your life experiences. How these are combined makes unique individuals.

Separating the Internal from the External

In learning how to handle anger (and other feelings), it is very important to separate external situations (what is happening in the world around us) from our internal reactions (what we feel about those situations). In many cases, *how we interpret a situation* determines whether or not we choose to get angry.

For example, if you are a young man and your girlfriend tells you that she values your friendship and would rather go back to that type of relationship, you can interpret this in at least two different ways.

You can say to yourself: "If she wants to break up with me, that's her choice. It's not a reflection on the kind of person I am. She has a right to make this choice. She really does value my friendship, and that's more important to her than having a more intimate relationship with me." You may still be sad, but you will not feel bad about yourself.

Or you might think: "She broke up with me because I haven't been a good enough boyfriend. I don't know what's wrong with me. I'm afraid that other girls may react the same way." If you interpret the event in this way, you will have negative thoughts about yourself, and you are likely to start to feel bad about yourself. You may get angry. Remember that negative thoughts or negative self-talk escalates anger.

In this case, there are two external facts: your girlfriend wants to have a friendship-based relationship with you, and she says that she does because she values your friendship so highly. The first interpretation is consistent with these facts, and it casts a positive light on the situation. The second interpretation is negative and destructive; furthermore, it doesn't fit the facts, unless you believe that your girlfriend is lying.

An Example with a Stranger

Consider this example. You are in a store looking at clothes and notice a stranger with what appears to be an angry look on his face. He seems to be looking in your direction.

Your first reaction might be to interpret this event in a personal way. You become uncomfortable; you may even start feeling angry at this person for giving *you* an angry look. You may start having negative thoughts, such as, "Who does he think he is looking at me like I'm nobody?" or "Who does he think he is messing with?"

Let's look at the external facts. A person whom you do not know has a look on his face that appears to be an angry look. That person is looking in your general direction. That's all we really know in this case. The internal interpretation that we just gave is consistent with the facts. It is entirely possible that this stranger is, for some unknown reason, angry with you.

It is more likely, however, that you have misinterpreted something. Perhaps the look on the stranger's face is not anger at all. It looks like anger, but could it be pain (he just had a root canal) or impatience (his wife had better hurry up if they are going to get to the movie on time). Even if it is an angry look, could it be that the stranger's anger is for some other person? He may be looking in your direction, but that doesn't mean he's looking at you. He may be looking at something or someone else near you, or he may be lost in his own thoughts and not be aware of you at all.

What you do will depend on how you see this situation. Why look for trouble? You have no needs that have to be met here. You can just tell yourself that the stranger has no reason to be angry with you, and walk away. What you feel you need and what you do about it depend on your point of view. *Your* point of view is entirely under *your* control.

▼

Your Friends Can Be Your Worst Enemies

Other people may also inadvertently influence the way you feel and think about an event. Suppose you are going to a ball game. While you are walking to your seat, someone bumps into you. Your internal evaluation is that it probably was an accident. The man could have stopped to tell you that he was sorry, but he didn't. This might make him rude, and you might be a little bit annoyed, but you can let go of that feeling. You are not likely to get mad or take action. Unless …

Now suppose that you are at the game with some friends. One of them, Barney, sees the bump and *he* responds with anger. He tells you that the other person bumped into you on purpose, to challenge you to a fight. Barney goes on to say that if you do not fight back, you will be a wimp. Do you think this might influence the way that you look at the event, how you feel, and what you do?

You might say "no way," but actually most of us *are* influenced by the way others see things. There are two reasons for this. First, you might be unsure of your own interpretation, so if your friend sees it differently, you might be tempted to assume that he is right. Second, even if Barney is probably wrong, you don't want him to think you're a wimp, regardless of the facts.

Before you take Barney's interpretation instead of your own, keep in mind that your friend may have personal issues that cause him to interpret a lot of behaviors as challenges. Barney might have a need to fight others; you do not. Barney may have an aggressive way of looking at the world; you are trying to develop an assertive way.

Think about what might happen depending on how you interpret the event. If you stick with your own interpretation, you find your seat and enjoy the ball game. If you take Barney's, you end up in a fight. Even if you win the fight, you still will have to use the ice in your soda to try to take some of the pain out of your swollen hands. Then your hands will still hurt, plus your soda will be warm. It's your choice.

▼

CHAPTER 6

THE PURPOSE OF ANGER

◀◀ UNIT 1 ▶▶

A NEW JOURNEY

The End of One Journey ...

There is an old song that goes like this:

> *The bear climbed over the mountain.*
> *The bear climbed over the mountain.*
> *The bear climbed over the mountain*
> *To see what he could see.*

You have been climbing a mountain. Your journey took you through recognition of your anger, bringing it under control, and using it effectively by assertive action. By getting to this point, you have climbed to the top of the mountain. One journey is finished. If you decide not to go any further in this workbook, you can still proudly say that you have learned important skills. You are able to prevent anger from hurting you (and others), and you are able to turn angry situations to your advantage.

Of course, if you quit now, you will never know what the bear saw after he climbed over the mountain.

... And the Start of Another

The song continues:

> *He saw another mountain.*
> *He saw another mountain.*
> *He saw another mountain*
> *And that is what he saw.*

Your first journey has taken you to the top of the Mountain of Control. From here, you can survey valleys and other mountains that can take you even further and higher. You can see the trail to another great peak—the Mountain of Problem Solving.

The rest of the workbook takes you on a second journey, or, more aptly, a continuation of your first, courageous journey.

How Many Mountains Are There?

Unlike the bear, who climbs one mountain only to see another mountain again and again, this workbook guides you on only two major journeys. As you proceed, you will see other trails leading to rivers, valleys, canyons, and mountains. When you reach the top of Mt. Problem Solving, you will find innumerable trails covering its slopes and leading off in all directions.

Exploring these trails is how you grow as a person. There is no end to them and no limit to your growth. By following this workbook, you not only are learning to harness and use anger, but you are also learning how to discover and follow some of the trails of your mind and heart that will inevitably lead you to a more satisfying life.

For now, however, we need to get ready for your second journey.

A Question for a Wise Man

Before you begin, however, you discover that Mt. Control is the home of a very wise man who is called simply "the Guru." Invited to ask one question of the Guru, you select this: "Now that I can control my anger, why do I need to go on a second journey?"

The Guru responds: "I will answer your question, but before I do, you must try to answer it for yourself." Since it is almost always a good idea to follow the advice of a Guru, I suggest that you think about possible answers before going on.

Here is the Guru's answer. "Think of an alarm clock that rings every time you are feeling bad. When you hear the ring, you must get up, go over to the alarm clock, and shut it off by pressing a button. Once this is done, you may go back to whatever you wish to do until the alarm clock rings again. Then you must get up once more, go to the alarm, and press the button. You must keep doing this over and over again. How much energy will you then have left for the rest of your life?"

As the Guru pauses for a drink of clear mountain water, you ponder his analogy. Anger is like the alarm clock. You have learned to shut it off by using AITs and assertive behavior, but doing so takes time and mental energy. There must be a better way, and, of course, the Guru will tell you what it is.

"How much better would it be," the Guru continues, "to prevent the alarms from sounding instead of having to respond to them? This is how you will benefit from the second journey." The Guru waves toward the lush green valley below and a winding river that flows through it, running off in the distance to its source on Mt. Problem Solving.

"This is the path you will travel," he says as he points to a winding road. "At the end of the journey, you will reach a mountain pass blocked by a magic door. To pass through, you will need several special tools, which can be found along the river road. You must begin your journey with high energy so that you are able to find and win these tools, for without them, you will never be able to reach the top of the mountain."

With that, the Guru closes his eyes and says no more. He has convinced you to begin the second journey, but you still have several questions. Since the Guru responds to only one question per customer, you will have to rely on your counselor and this workbook for your other answers.

Preparing for the Journey

Your first is: "What did the Guru mean by starting with high energy?". It sounds like a video game A game character who runs out of energy usually gets destroyed by one of the dangers of the game. Sometimes you can get more energy along the way, but it's a good idea to start with as much as possible. Where do you get this energy?

Actually, you get it from your anger. Unit 3 will tell you all about it.

Another question you might have is: "What are these tools I will need and how will I find them?" No problem. This workbook will be your guide and will point out the tools to you as you come across them in the rest of this chapter and in Chapter 7.

If you ask how easy it will be to find the right path, I will have to be truthful and tell you that the path is faint in places and may be hard to follow. You might even get lost. By this I mean that you might find one or two of the units difficult to understand the first time you read them. Fortunately, getting lost in this workbook has easy remedies—you can ask your counselor for help, or, if you want to do it yourself, you can start the unit over again!

Finally, you might ask if you can take someone along with you. The answer is that you not only may, but you must. Your counselor will always be there. You may also want to proceed through the rest of this workbook with a friend or helper (or even two or three, if they are available).

◄◄ UNIT 2 ►►
THE LOOK AND FEEL OF ANGER

Before we begin our journey, we need to load up on energy. But where do we find it? Since the only things we have brought with us so far are anger and the tools to manage it, that is where we need to look.

The Images of Anger

First, we will examine the anger itself, searching for something within it that we can use to provide the emotional energy we need for the tasks ahead. Let's start by looking at how anger, as a *feeling*, is usually perceived in our society.

Anger evokes vivid images. When people are asked to identify characters who remind them of anger, they may mention Rambo, the Incredible Hulk, or Charles Manson. Charles Manson represents anger at its worst, whereas the Incredible Hulk and Rambo are more benign. Why do you think people see Manson differently from the Hulk and Rambo?

Part of the answer may be that what Charles Manson *did* with his anger was evil. Rambo and the Hulk only hurt the "bad guys." They served the purposes of justice. Even though he represented pure and uncontrolled anger, the Incredible Hulk always seemed to know who were the good guys and who were the bad guys. Furthermore, he never hurt anyone severely, even the bad guys.

What does anger "look like"? When I ask children to tell me what they think anger looks like, many of them say, "Monsters." For some children, anger represents an ugly, unrecognizable, and unlovable image in a parent. When people get angry, their face muscles may contract in various ways, resulting in scary distortions. It is difficult for young children to see love in anger. Both children and adults often see the face of anger as a very frightening image.

ASSIGNMENT 33

Directions:

1. What visual images do you get when you say the word "anger"? An example might be: "Someone on the ground, hurt and bleeding." If you have trouble thinking of images, you can review your anger journal and find some there. Write these down in your notebook.

2. Name some angry people. Write these in your notebook. Try to get at least one each of real people, characters on television, characters in movies, and characters in books.

3. In your notebook, write down as many common phrases as you can think of that use the word "anger" or "angry" (for example, "angry storm" or "red with anger").

4. For each set of items below, rank them in order of how "angry" they seem to you:

    a. Tornado, thunderstorm, shower

    b. Deer, fox, wolf

    c. Blue, red, white

COMMENTS ON ASSIGNMENT 33

In answer to question 4, most people would give these rankings:

a. Tornado, thunderstorm, shower. The tornado is visualized as being the angriest because it is the most destructive.

b. Wolf, fox, deer. The wolf seems angriest because it is thought of as the most violent.

c. Red, white, blue. Red is perceived as the color of anger because it is the hottest, and thus the most intense.

The images that anger evokes are often violent, destructive, and intense. This makes anger an ideal emotion for television and the movies—it keeps the viewer interested. When you think of angry characters (even "good" ones, such as Rambo and the Hulk), you probably recognize the intensity that often goes with this emotion. For example, in episodes of the Incredible Hulk, the intensity of the Hulk's emotion depended on the size of the wrong that was done. This may have been an attempt to justify his behavior. Clearly, there is a lot of energy in the emotion "anger." Unit 3 shows you how to capture it and use it to meet your own needs.

SUMMARY: Anger contains a lot of energy, and energy is just what you need to make the most of your anger!

◀◀ UNIT 3 ▶▶
CHANNELING THE ENERGY OF ANGER

Anger Is Like a Flood

Think of anger as a flood of uncontrolled emotions. It rages unchecked through a mountain valley, but you have learned to build a dam to stop that flood. You use AITs for that purpose. Once you have stopped the flood, you can channel it in a direction of your own choosing.

Letting It Go

Once you have your anger under control, there are two things you can do with it. You can just "let it go," or you can use its energy to do something positive for yourself.

Sometimes, letting it go is the better choice. This is the case when there is really nothing you *can* do, or when taking any action is not worth the gain that might result. Consider what happened to James on his second day at home after leaving the institution.

James had decided to go back to school, but he wanted a part-time job so that he would have a little spending money. A fast-food restaurant in his neighborhood was hiring, so James went in to fill out an application. While he was leaning on the counter writing, a five- or six-year old boy, peering over the counter to see what James was doing, dripped ice cream on the application.

James' first inclination was to become angry, but he was practiced enough to keep his anger under control. He would have told the boy's mother that she should control her son, but he noticed that she was trying hard to keep tabs on a younger boy and was carrying a baby. It just wasn't worth saying anything to her. James could easily get another application and fill it out on a higher counter.

That is just what he did. That would be the end of this story, except for a happy coincidence. The manager of the restaurant saw the entire incident. He knew of James' reputation for temper and probably would not have hired him, but the way in which James handled the incident with the ice cream was just what he was looking for in an employee. So James got the job. For once, a good deed brought its own reward.

Not Letting It Go

In many cases, however, letting it go is a waste. You went to all of the trouble to harness the power of the flood by building a dam, and you should be able to use that power. The way to do this seems simple:

1. Decide what you want to accomplish.
2. Figure out how to accomplish it.
3. Take the necessary actions.

Each of these steps at times can be difficult. It is not always obvious what you want to accomplish. Determining how to do it often is even harder. Taking the necessary actions may require a lot of self-discipline, or even courage.

Delayed Actions

Sometimes action must be delayed. This may be because you need time to decide what to do and how to do it. Or it may be because the actions you need to take cannot be carried out immediately. In this case, you want to store the energy you feel as a result of the anger. You want to be able to use it later.

There is a bottle in which such energy can be stored. It has a label with large blue letters that spell "RESOLVE." (Some people say that their bottles are titled "DETERMINATION.")

I knew a 15-year old boy, Eddie, who played on his high-school soccer team. He was a fair player, and since his team had only a few reserves, he got a lot of playing time. During one important game, the other team scored a goal that the coach thought Eddie should have prevented. Actually, it wasn't Eddie's fault—his own teammate had accidentally tripped him just as Eddie moved to stop the opposing player. The coach, however, didn't see the trip and so thought Eddie had missed the play.

At the next time-out, the coach called Eddie over and "chewed him out." Eddie was angry. He wanted to tell the coach it wasn't his fault. He thought the coach should not criticize someone before hearing all of the facts. He wanted the coach to apologize, but just then the whistle blew, restarting the game, and Eddie had to hustle back to his position.

Eddie could have just let the matter go, but he decided that he would talk to the coach after the game. So he took the energy of his anger, put it into the RESOLVE bottle, and finished the game. When the game was over, Eddie was tired. It would have been easy just to forget the entire matter, but Eddie had RESOLVE. Remembering how he felt when he had bottled the energy, Eddie showered and dressed and then sought out the coach.

The result was anticlimactic. The other player had already told the coach what had happened. As soon as the coach saw Eddie, he apologized. He even said that he shouldn't have been so quick to jump to a conclusion. Eddie got what he needed without using the energy in the RESOLVE bottle, but it was there if he had needed it.

When to Close the Bottle

What exactly do I mean by opening the RESOLVE bottle and using its energy? It's really nothing more than remembering how you felt when the energy from your anger was fresh in your mind. By recalling these feelings, you can retrieve that energy when it can be put to good use.

It is very important to close the RESOLVE bottle at the right time. You want positive energy in the bottle, so you do not want to close it when your anger is still uncontrolled. If you did that, opening the bottle would just make you angry again. You need to close the bottle after you bring your anger under control, and after you decide that you want to take some action, but that you can't do it right away.

Suppose your older brother roars out of the driveway at high speed, almost hitting you. You have to dive out of the way of the screeching tires. You are quite upset. Let's bottle your feelings at this instant and call that bottle 1.

Your brother has already sped away. You get up and dust yourself off. This is not the first time this has happened. You need to do something about it. Your anger is under control, you have decided to act, and you have even decided what that action will be. When you next see your brother, you are going to have a very serious talk with him. Let's close bottle 2 now.

The next morning, you see your brother at the breakfast table. You have a bottle of RESOLVE in your pocket and now is the time to open it. If it is bottle 1 that you open, you remember the squeal of the tires, the pain of your fall, and the rage you felt at that moment. You reach over the table and punch your brother in the eye. This results in a full-fledged fight. The table is turned on end, dishes are broken, both you and your brother end up with cuts and bruises, and nothing is resolved. You and your brother do, however, get the privilege of paying $122 to cover the damages.

On the other hand, if you open bottle 2, you remember that you had decided to have a serious talk with your brother. You don't want this to happen again. So you tell him how you feel; he explains that he was late for work; you tell him that running over you is not worth saving two seconds; he apologizes; and maybe he will be more careful next time.

Which bottle would you want to open? (Hint: This is not a trick question.)

Not an Assignment

There is no assignment at this point. For the next 5 or 10 days, however, try to bottle your energy whenever you can. Whenever there is some action you must take, or some problem you must solve, put that RESOLVE away in a bottle. Then make sure that you open it at the proper time and take the action you need to take. Use your anger journal to record when you close a bottle of RESOLVE, and when you open and use it. You may be surprised at how much better you feel about yourself. Score one point for each time you bottle your energy and two more each time you open the bottle and use the energy effectively. Can you score 20 points in a week?

◄◄ UNIT 4 ►►
FEELINGS

Feelings Are Part of Life

The ability to *feel* is part of almost everyone's experience as a human being. Does this mean that we are constantly feeling strong emotions? The answer is "No." In fact, sometimes we may not be feeling anything at all. But each of us has the ability to experience feelings.

For example: what are you feeling when you first wake up in the morning? Imagine just waking up, before you even get out of bed. As you open your eyes, does any remarkable or strong feeling come to mind? If you are very relaxed, stretching on your bed, a small smile might creep onto your face. But are you feeling anything? Take a moment to think about this question before reading the next paragraph.

If you are imagining a situation like the one I have in mind, you probably said that you were feeling happy, or perhaps relaxed, calm, content, or just "good." The feeling may not be a very strong one, but even in this first waking moment, you are experiencing feelings.

Of course, circumstances surrounding your life may contribute to your waking feelings. When James woke up in the institution, he was confronted by a 10-by-10 windowless room, with a toilet in the corner, and a few belongings neatly stacked in a box. Do you think his first feelings were happy ones?

The Good, the Bad, and the So-So

If someone asked you right now, while you are reading this workbook, how you were feeling, you might not even take the question seriously. You are not feeling much of anything right now. If you did answer, it would probably be something like "Okay."

Most of the time, you feel this way. You say you are feeling "normal," meaning that you are not experiencing any strong or remarkable emotions. You are not feeling as good or as relaxed as you do when you first wake up, so you would not say "happy." We do not try to analyze these "normal" everyday feelings, but rather just experience them. The feelings that need further attention are the ones you experience very intensely, particularly those that are very uncomfortable.

SUMMARY: Feeling "okay" is okay. Feeling "good" is okay. Not feeling much of anything is okay. Feeling bad and uncomfortable is *not* okay. Which of these feelings do you need to do something about?

We might feel happiness intensely, but happiness does not make us uncomfortable. Therefore, very few people would find it necessary to do anything more about the feeling of happiness than simply to enjoy it. However, the feelings that interfere with our ability to function or enjoy life do warrant attention.

It may be simplistic, but we can divide our feelings into "bad," "okay," and "good." This does not mean that we are bad or wrong for having "bad" feelings. It means that "bad" feelings make us feel bad.

There are a very large number of words that people use to describe their feelings. You might not be able to think of many of them immediately, but if you take some time, you can probably list 50 or 100 "feelings." Two words sometimes describe the same feeling or feelings that are so close that you can't easily tell the difference between them.

For example, "disappointed" and "uneasy" are bad feelings, whereas "accomplishment" and "joy" are good feelings, or feelings that make us feel good.

ASSIGNMENT 34

Directions:

1. In the following Feelings Frame, list up to 10 "good" feelings and 10 "bad" ones. If you can't think of 10, try to have at least five or six in each column.

2. Ask a friend to do the same thing in the second Feelings Frame. If you can get a number of people to fill out Feelings Frames, so much the better. Your counselor can give you extra frames, or you can just use paper from your notebook.

3. Compare lists. How many feelings appear on two or more lists? Are there cases where the same feeling is described using different words?

FEELINGS FRAME

PERSON FILLING OUT THIS FRAME	
FEELINGS THAT FEEL GOOD	**FEELINGS THAT FEEL BAD**

FEELINGS FRAME

PERSON FILLING OUT THIS FRAME	
FEELINGS THAT FEEL GOOD	FEELINGS THAT FEEL BAD

◄◄ **UNIT 5** ►►

ANGER AS A FEELING

Is Anger a Good or a Bad Feeling?

Did anyone who filled out a Feelings Frame list anger as a feeling? If so, was it shown as a good feeling or as a bad one? The first inclination is to say that anger is a bad feeling, because it is uncomfortable and often leads to bad results. James would surely agree. On the other hand, Sharon might say that anger can be a good feeling, because it helped her free herself from an intolerable situation.

This observation—that anger can sometimes be a good feeling and sometimes be a bad feeling—is a hint that anger is different from other feelings. Some people think (and I agree) that anger is not a *primary emotion* at all—but is a reaction to other emotions.

Sharon Lashes Out at a Friend

Let's examine something that happened to Sharon. It had been a year since she and Clark had filed for divorce and the final papers had just arrived. As soon as Sharon signed them and delivered them to the court, her divorce would be final. A few of her friends happened to be in the room at the time. One of them tried to be sympathetic, saying, "Oh, this must be a very difficult time for you."

Uncharacteristically, Sharon showed her anger at this statement. She had been trying for months to learn to express anger, and this time she succeeded admirably. "What are you talking about? This is a great moment for me. I couldn't be happier!" Then she caught herself and looked embarrassed.

She apologized for her outburst and gave this explanation. "I really needed to get out of the relationship with Clark, but it was still an important part of my life. There have been so many changes in the last year. I'm really not sure where I'm going and how things will end up. These papers make the end of my old life so *final*."

Why did Sharon get angry at her friend's sympathetic comment? Think about this for a moment before reading on.

I think that Sharon had been keeping her uncertainties about her future locked up, much as she had locked away her anger with Clark. She had been trying not to think about loneliness, financial insecurity, and how she would react to other men, among many other issues. When her friend said that this was "a difficult time," those walls broke. Sharon came face-to-face with feelings of insecurity, uncertainty, and maybe even inadequacy. These made her *very* uncomfortable. To avoid these bad feelings, Sharon got angry.

Being angry was less uncomfortable for Sharon than were the feelings that triggered the anger. Anger was a messenger, telling Sharon that something was wrong. Anger was also a shield, hiding more difficult feelings.

Sharon was able to control her anger and then quickly discover the feelings that lay behind it. She apologized to her friend, and even was able to speak to us about those underlying feelings. But this is often very hard to do.

Anger as a Messenger

Surely, one of the purposes that anger serves is as a messenger—it tells you that "something is wrong." Once you have controlled the anger and taken such immediate actions as necessary to deal with the threat, you are left with this "something is wrong" message. Before you can bottle your angry energy by deciding to act, you have to know what is wrong.

It might have been easy for Sharon to say that she got angry because her friend had made a false statement about her. Of course, if she closed the RESOLVE bottle there, her later action might be never to see her friend again. That would take care of the problem of false statements. Sharon would have solved a problem, but, unfortunately, it would not have been the right problem to solve.

Sharon realized, however, that this angry feeling was a messenger, so she thought more deeply about what was really wrong. In the end, it allowed her to unmask the real problem and (over the next several months) to deal with it effectively.

Ignoring the Messenger

So far in this workbook, we have been treating anger as if it were a primary emotion. The AITs were learned to allow you to control the anger. Assertive behavior let you get some of your needs met almost at once. This process is useful, but it ignores anger's role as a messenger.

Ignoring a messenger might be acceptable once in a while, but there are people who make a habit of it. For them, anger is an all-consuming feeling that prevents them from experiencing other feelings. They see life through a fog of anger. For these people, anger is devastating in that it interferes with their chance for living a normal life and having opportunities for happiness.

We often call them "angry people" since they seem angry most of the time. If you have seen an "angry person," you have probably seen this person's pain. Anger hurts. Long-term anger hurts more. If you know an angry person, you undoubtedly have noticed that person using a lot of energy to battle emotions and the world in general. An angry person is constantly at war, because seeing the world through angry eyes blinds one to the peaceful, happy side of life.

One of the problems with people who are angry all the time is that they may have grown used to being and living angry, and may not even identify their combative style of relating to the world as anger. So the anger becomes a way of life, a way they are used to feeling, rather than a message that something is wrong. Without this message, there is no positive force for change. Anger in this situation is not power, but a heavy, useless burden.

Every time you ignore the messenger "anger," you are becoming a little bit like an angry person. For me, that is reason enough to keep a sharp lookout for the messenger and to try very hard to understand the message.

What is this message anyway? The next unit shows you how to find out.

◄◄ UNIT 6 ►►
THE MESSAGE OF ANGER

Anger Is a Shield

Suppose you are in a situation in which something happens that makes you feel very uncomfortable. For example, a friend starts talking about a young man you had dated previously—in front of your current boyfriend. Before you can stop her, she blurts out that she saw the two of you together last night. You feel embarrassed and very guilty. These emotions make you feel bad, so you cover them up with an especially intense anger. The angry feeling is hiding the embarrassment and guilt. Since the angry feeling is not as bad for you as the ones it is hiding, you feel better.

It all makes good sense. Why not use anger to feel better? By now you know the answer to that question. You know that your angry actions can cause you a great deal more pain than the embarrassment and guilt would have caused. Now you can also see that by letting the anger take over, you are hiding your real emotions.

If these emotions are hidden, how can you deal with them?

The Advantages of Discovery

Suppose you strip away the anger and reveal the underlying embarrassment and guilt. Now you feel worse again—the relief the anger gave you is gone, like pain returning after the aspirin wears off. What have you gained?

The answer is that you have taken the first, and necessary, step toward solving the real problem. In this case, the real problem is that you have not been honest with your current boyfriend. Further, you have been caught. What should you do about it?

This is a classic case for problem solving, and that is the destination of your current journey. The first step, however, is defining the problem. By discovering the emotions beneath your anger, you have been able to define the problem clearly. Now you at least have a chance to do something about it.

Speed Masks the Deed

When something happens to you, the resulting feelings may appear very quickly. You may not have time to give conscious meaning to the event. Such feelings as hurt, embarrassment, shame, guilt, fear, or surprise, sometimes quite intense and uncomfortable, may appear in an instant. Because these feelings are very uncomfortable, you may translate them into an angry feeling before you even know that you have them.

In short, it can all happen so quickly that you don't see and can't remember the transition from other emotions to anger. Looking back on it, you might be tempted to deny that you felt anything except anger. Sometimes you have to dig deep into your heart to understand what really happened.

It can be difficult to find the emotions behind the anger. This makes the assignment at the end of the unit very important. Please pay special attention to it, and keep recording your underlying emotions for at least a full week.

A Clue, a Clue, My Kingdom for a Clue

There is a clue that sometimes helps you ferret out your real emotions. Consider the intensity of your anger. Intense anger (high numbers on your Anger Scale) comes from emotions that are especially uncomfortable.

In the example at the beginning of this unit, you got very angry. In examining the situation later, you might say that your anger was due to embarrassment. But the embarrassment wasn't a bad enough feeling to account for the intensity of your anger. There must have been something else. Digging deeper, you recall the feeling of guilt, and maybe also a feeling of being betrayed (by your friend).

This is a good rule to follow: "Don't stop digging until you have hit enough paydirt to explain the intensity of the anger you felt."

Revisiting the Intervention Model

In Chapter 3, you were introduced to an Intervention Model. This was for the purpose of learning to control your anger. To refresh your memory, the model can be summarized in these three steps:

1. Recognize your anger.

2. Evaluate the threat.

3. Take an action to control the anger (use an AIT).

The Problem-Solving Model also comprises three steps:

1. Recognize anger as a messenger emotion.

2. Define the problem by discovering the true, underlying emotions.

3. Solve the problem.

Actually, the third step—"solve the problem"—in the Problem-Solving Model is more than one step. We can use this simplification, however, to see an interesting parallel between the two models. They both start with recognizing something. The second step is figuring out what the threat or problem is. The third step is taking the action necessary to meet the threat or solve the problem. Figure 7 illustrates these models.

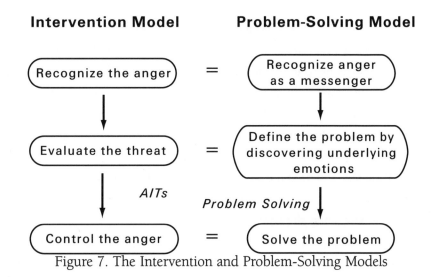

Figure 7. The Intervention and Problem-Solving Models

It's Always Easier the Second Time Around

It is not by accident that the Intervention Model and the Problem-Solving Model are so similar. Controlling anger is actually an example of problem solving! The same techniques that you learned in Chapters 2 through 5 to control your anger are now going to be applied to the wider task of solving all types of problems. You mastered these techniques once; the second time won't be hard at all!

ASSIGNMENT 35

Directions:

1. For each of the situations described below, select the emotions that probably are underlying the anger. Write the answers in your notebook.

A. Serena is angry. Her mother searched her room without her permission and found cigarettes. Then her mother and her father started yelling at her, telling her that she was too young to smoke. What did they know? She was almost 13. She could do what she wanted to.

B. Josh is angry. His car broke down again and he can't afford to have it fixed. Without his car, Josh doesn't know how he can get to work on time. And without a job, there is no way he can ever fix his car.

C. Claudette is angry. She has just been stood up by her date. Now she won't be able to go to the senior prom, and all of her friends are going to wonder why.

You can look at the comments following this assignment before going on to the next direction.

2. Pick several real-life or television situations in which a character displays anger and identify the underlying emotions. If possible, do this with one or more friends while watching an hour or so of television.

COMMENTS ON ASSIGNMENT 35

A. Serena feels *embarrassed* and *guilty* about being caught with cigarettes, because she knows her parents don't allow her to smoke. She also feels *betrayed*, since she feels that her parents violated her privacy by searching her room.

B. Josh's main feeling is *frustration*. He is in a situation for which he can find no good solution. He is also feeling *insecure* because he now doesn't know whether or not he can keep his job.

C. Claudette is *disappointed* not to go to the prom. She also is *insecure*, since she doesn't know why she has been stood up. Could it be her fault? She is *uncertain* about what to say when she sees her friends.

You may have found other emotions in these situations; the answers I gave are by no means the only correct ones.

Pick Up Your Tool

You have now been led to where your first tool is lying by the path. It looks like a magnifying glass and you use it like one—to see things that could not be seen without it. The tool is your ability to discover the emotions that cause and underlie your anger. Assignment 36 will help you pick up that tool.

▼

ASSIGNMENT 36

Directions:

1. For at least the next week, use your anger journal to note any time you become even slightly angry. In each case, describe what happened and try to identify your underlying emotions. This is a very important assignment, so do it with care.

▼

CHAPTER 7

VALUES AND NEEDS

Two More Tools

The path to Mt. Problem Solving now takes a curious turn. Up until this point, we have been discussing anger. In this chapter, the words "anger" and "angry" do not even appear (after this sentence).

Instead, you will be led to two important tools: understanding your *values* and understanding your *needs*. These, together with the tool of understanding your *feelings* that you picked up at the end of the last chapter, are the ones you will need in Chapter 8.

What Are Values?

Let's start with values. Values are the beliefs that we have about the world, and the importance we give to these beliefs. Honesty is an example of a value. You may believe that honesty is very important, and because you value honesty, you usually will behave honestly.

The last sentence seems obvious, doesn't it? Read it again. The crucial idea here is that your value (honesty) causes you to act in a certain way (honestly). *What you do depends to a great extent on what you believe.*

I think you can convince yourself that this is true. For example, Matthew had a strong value of patriotism. One day, Matthew and some friends passed a park where a political demonstration was taking place. Some of the demonstrators were burning an American flag. The instant he saw this, Matthew charged at the flag burners, grabbed the flag, and beat out the flames. Several of the larger demonstrators surrounded Matthew. Fortunately, Matthew's friends intervened and he escaped unharmed. The demonstrators went back to burning the flag.

▼

The Cost of Acting Against Your Values

Why did Matthew risk personal harm to rescue a piece of cloth? If you were to ask him later, he would say: "I know it was silly and I shouldn't have done it, but I just felt I had to." Matthew is telling us that if he had not acted, he would have felt bad. He would have been anxious and uncomfortable. We know from the last chapter that uncomfortable people try to do something to relieve their distress. In this case, Matthew risked life and limb to get rid of the uncomfortable (bad) feeling that he had when he saw the flag being burned.

The cost for Matthew to act against his value of patriotism would have been to feel rotten. This was the motivation that caused him to charge the demonstrators.

I don't think you are any different. If you solve a problem by doing something that contradicts your values, you end up feeling bad. You may even feel worse than you did with the original problem. On the other hand, if you know your values, you can pick a course of action that supports them.

A Person with No Values

Every person has a set of values. Values are a way of measuring what a person feels is right or wrong, good or bad. You may have heard people say about someone: "He has no values." What this really means is that this person is behaving in a way that does not reflect what is important to him.

For example, Penny stole a CD from a music store, and then told her mother that her friend Nancy had given it to her. When Nancy denied it, Penny was caught, but she refused to take responsibility for her action, saying, "The store doesn't need the money anyway." It's tempting to believe that nothing is important to Penny—that she has no values. Relationships must not be important to her, because she lies to people. Community must not be important, because she steals from others.

Does Penny really lack values? Probably not. There are several reasons why Penny might be actions the way she does. Perhaps she has values that are different from those that most of us hold—values that don't prevent her from stealing or lying. Perhaps she has values that would prohibit such actions but carried them out anyway because of other values or circumstances.

I'm not trying to excuse Penny's behavior. What I'm saying is that you can't get out of the assignments in this chapter by saying you don't have any values. You do.

◄◄ UNIT 2 ►►
A LIST OF VALUES

There are probably hundreds of values that are held by one person or another, but if you had to make a list of them now, how many could you name? Try it—it may be harder than you think. To help you along, I will describe a few values in this unit.

Values Concerning the Individual

Values that have to do with individuals and being human include:

▶ *Survival*. Most of us value our own existence very highly. We will do almost anything to stay alive.

▶ *Freedom*. The ability to make one's own choices is something for which many people have fought and died.

▶ *Honor*. It might be easy to cheat on a test, but a lot of people don't do it because it would offend their sense of honor.

▶ *Knowledge*. The quest for knowledge is all-consuming for some people, while others don't seem to care much about it.

▶ *Chivalry*. In some societies, chivalry is such a strong value that men will die rather than violate it.

Moral Values

As an individual, you may also have moral values. These are your beliefs about what is right and what is wrong. Some examples are:

▶ *Responsibility*. We often hear people lament that others do not take responsibility for their actions, but instead blame their behaviors on others.

▶ *Honesty*. One of the 10 Commandments is, "Thou shalt not lie," but honesty is a value held very strongly by some and hardly at all by others.

▶ *Dependability*. Your boss will probably tell you this is a very important value, but will he or she demonstrate the value himself or herself?

Social Values

Social values are those that are important to us in relation to society, such as:

▶ *Justice*. "It isn't fair!" is a complaint that almost all of us have voiced at one time or another, showing our value of justice.

▶ *Peace*. Possibly linked to survival, the yearning for peace is an almost universal value.

▶ *Cooperation*. Working together can produce much better results than those available to individuals, so cooperation is often held in high esteem.

▶ *Sharing*. When we say that it makes us feel good to share something with others, we are expressing the strength of our sharing value.

▶ *Tolerance*. Although nobody wants to be called "intolerant," many people are, showing that they lack this value.

The values described in this unit are just a small sample. You can probably think of many others.

▼

ASSIGNMENT 37

Directions:

1. Use the following Values Frame to list 10 of your most important values. These are the ones you hold the most strongly. (If you can't think of 10, list as many as you can.)

2. Have a friend fill out a Values Frame. Compare your values with your friend's. If you can, have several other people fill out Values Frames and compare everyone's lists. Your counselor can supply you with extra Values Frames.

VALUES FRAME

TOP 10 LIST OF VALUES FOR . . .	
NUMBER	**VALUE**
1	
2	
3	
4	
5	
6	
7	
8	
9	
10	

▼

VALUES FRAME

TOP 10 LIST OF VALUES FOR . . .	
NUMBER	**VALUE**
1	
2	
3	
4	
5	
6	
7	
8	
9	
10	

◀◀ UNIT 3 ▶▶
HOW VALUES DIFFER

Values in Different Groups of People

You may have noticed that different groups of people have different values. For example, people living in other countries often have values that are different from ours. You may value competition, whereas people from a different culture would prefer cooperation.

Even among people in the same country, values may differ. If you are part of a group, your values will probably be similar to those of other people in your group. People who share the same culture or religion often have very similar values and beliefs.

Misunderstandings

These differences in values can lead to misunderstandings. If we believe that something is very important, we might also believe that to be true for everybody. When others do not hold the same belief, it can be very frustrating to try to communicate. Because our values are so important to us, we forget that other people may hold different values, and that what we think of as very important, they may consider to be of small value. We might even think that the person who does not agree with us is not listening to us. In reality, he or she may be listening very well, but because of different values, might not agree with us.

Differences in values sometimes lead to major conflicts, as we have seen throughout history. Sometimes when people have different values, they may see their values as being "right" or "correct," and other people's values as "wrong." Situations like these can easily lead to major misunderstandings, and even war.

Can Values Be "Right"?

Can a value be "right" or "wrong"? This is a difficult question. Most people would say that "honesty" is right. They would also say that "loyalty" is right. But which of the two is more important? On that point, there is a lot of disagreement. Even if some values are held by almost everyone, and, therefore, appear to be "right," exactly how important that value is will always be in question.

Consider James and his latest girlfriend, Janice. One afternoon, James was standing near Janice's car, waiting for her. His best friend, Alan, drove by. As Alan leaned out the window to talk to James, his foot slipped off the brake and his car hit Janice's. It only scratched it, but the scratch was quite noticeable. Alan saw Janice approaching in the distance, told James not to say anything, and sped off.

When Janice saw the scratch on her car, she asked James what had caused it. He said that he didn't know, and that the scratch was there when he arrived. Unfortunately for James, one of Janice's other friends saw the whole thing and told her what had happened, including the fact that James was there at the time.

Janice was furious at James for lying to her, but James just said that he couldn't "rat" on a friend. Janice said, "But I'm your friend, too—you can't lie to me." James replied, "But Alan is my friend, too." The result—James is now free to find a different girlfriend.

It you were to ask James whether honesty was important, he would say "Yes." If you were to ask him why he had lied to Janice, he would say that loyalty was more important. Janice would tell you that honesty was more important. Who is right?

This situation did not have to end up in a fight between James and Janice. If each had understood that the other held different values, and had acted according to those values, they would have been able to work out their differences. But James thought he was "right" and that Janice just didn't understand. And Janice thought that she was "right," and felt very hurt that James would lie to her.

I think it is best to consider values as personal things that are neither "right" nor "wrong." Understanding your own values will help you make decisions. Tolerating other people's values will help you to understand their actions and to get along with them without conflict.

Differing Values Within a Family

There may be major differences in values even within families. These can lead to misunderstandings, miscommunication, and serious conflicts.

For example, when you were in your teens, independence might have been very important to you.

You valued making your own decisions; therefore, these decisions were influenced by your value of independence. At one time or another, we all do something we don't really want to do, just to prove that we have the right to make our own decisions.

At the same time, the adults probably valued loyalty and cooperation very highly, at least within the family. They expected everyone to make decisions for the good of the family, and to support those decisions regardless of personal feelings. The adults might have agreed that independence is important, but you felt much more strongly about it. In fact, you might even have thought that you valued independence so highly that cooperation in the family would mean compromising your independence.

Neither side was wrong, although this difference in what you and the family considered most important presented a major conflict. Because of their values, the adults may place expectations on a teenager that the teenager is not willing to meet. For example, they may ask the teen to spend more time with the family than he or she is willing to spend.

James often said that his parents didn't let him have enough independence. At the same time, however, his remarks indicated that he expected his parents to continue to live by their values of sharing, cooperation, and loyalty toward him. Because these were the values James held, he thought he was "right." James had not yet learned to look at events from other people's viewpoints, and he did not understand others' values well.

Here's the Tool

Hopefully, you will learn to recognize not only your own values, but also those of other people. In any situation of conflict, you should try to understand which of your values is affected. If you can do this, you will have picked up another tool—the ability to see how various things you might do will agree (or disagree) with your values. If you also can understand the values of other people, you will be able to recognize why they are acting the way that they are. This knowledge will help you find choices that "work" in the way you want them to work.

ASSIGNMENT 38

Directions:

1. The men and women of the 1960s who protested so strongly against the Vietnam war were expressing their values. These were in conflict with those of many of the members of the government, and of a large number of other Americans, who had decided to go to war and who felt it was right to continue it. This was a time of great conflict, often turning parent against child and husband against wife. What values are so strong that people would break up their families, and even leave their country, because of them? Use the following War Values Table to make a list of values that would contribute to a decision to go to war, and those that would contribute to a decision to end it.

2. After you have completed this list, take a separate piece of paper and rank these values. Which of the 10 values that you listed is most important to you? Which is second most important, and which is third?

3. Try to find one or more people who were at least 30 years old at the time of the war. Show them your table of values and ask them to name the most important three of the group. Do these rankings agree with yours?

WAR VALUES TABLE

GOING-TO-WAR LIST	NOT-GOING-TO-WAR LIST
1.	1.
2.	2.
3.	3.
4.	4.
5.	5.

◄◄ UNIT 4 ►►
BUILDING A NEW SOCIETY

This entire unit is really a large assignment. You will be led step-by-step to create your own society powered by your values. The purpose of this exercise is to help you really understand what your values are and where they may lead you. The assignment is long but very important. Take as much time as you need to complete it. It is definitely *not* considered cheating to have others help you with this unit. Discuss any part of it with anyone you please, but in the end use *your own* values to set up this new society.

A Fantastic Discovery

NASA has just discovered another planet, much like the earth, orbiting a nearby (astronomically speaking) star. The planet is inhabited by plants and animals, none of which have intelligence. Participants in several previous missions constructed buildings and have left all of the tools needed by a colony. They have returned to the earth, and now it is time to send the first permanent inhabitants.

You have been chosen to head the mission, and will be allowed to pick six people to go with you. Many more will follow later, but the initial group will set up the new society and decide how it will work. What kind of people will you choose to go with you? For the purpose of this exercise, don't worry about physical needs, such as including a doctor or an agricultural scientist. You can assume that they will come later. The people you pick will define the kind of society that will be created. You and they will decide what type of government will come into being. You will also create the other institutions—religious, political, economic, and social.

▼

Defining the Values of the New Society

As a first step, decide what values will be used as a base for the new society.

ASSIGNMENT 39

Directions:

1. Name the new planet. Be serious; the planet's name is important. If you give it a foolish name, it will be harder to recruit colonists.

2. List the individual, moral, and social values that you want your new society to embody. You can review Unit 2 to get some ideas. Write these values in the Types of Values Table that follows this assignment. You don't have to fill the table completely; on the other hand, if you need more space, that's fine (just use any other piece of paper).

3. Take a look at your list of values. Do you now want to change the name of your planet?

TYPES OF VALUES TABLE

INDIVIDUAL VALUES	MORAL VALUES	SOCIAL VALUES

Choosing the Colonists

Now that you have an idea of the values you want to instill in your new society, it is time to select your crew.

ASSIGNMENT 40

Directions:

1. Pick six people to go with you to help you set up the institutions of the new society. Use Crew Member Evaluation Forms like the following—one for each crew member. You may choose people you know, or fictional characters, or you can just invent people. By the way, there is nothing magical about six people; if you want to have one or two more or less, that's okay, too. Ask your counselor for the number of extra forms you will need (or make copies in your notebook).

CREW MEMBER EVALUATION FORM

Name:

Describe the person's abilities and personal characteristics—what kind of person is this?

What will this person do in the new society?

How will this person contribute toward instilling the values you have chosen in the new society?

◄◄ UNIT 5 ►►
NEEDS

What Are "Needs"?

"Needs" are things that are necessary for our physical and emotional well-being. Values and needs are closely related; in fact, some people think that values develop out of needs. But whereas values may be different for each person, everybody has much the same needs.

Physical Needs and Emotional Needs

Among our physical needs are: food, water, air, and sleep. Everyone, regardless of his or her values, has these needs.

Emotional needs are less obvious. Two basic ones are safety and security. These have to do with our ability to function, and even with our survival. You might say that shelter is a physical need, but it also is an emotional one. People need to have shelter in order to feel safe and secure.

Safety and security are considered basic needs, because they also have to do with our survival and our ability to function. People need to have shelter and to feel safe in order to meet their responsibilities. The types of shelter that people have differ greatly, ranging from the homeless person's cardboard box to the mansions that we only see from a distance. But the need for shelter, safety, and security is basic and is shared by everyone.

Some other emotional needs are love, caring, being part of a group or family, feeling good about yourself, learning, feeling important, having personal power, and finding a meaning or purpose in life. You might think you can live without these things, but it would be a bare existence. Your emotional well-being is dependent on getting these needs met.

Needs and Wants

Although everyone has the same needs, we go about meeting those needs in different ways. John and Richard both have the need for love. John is trying to meet that need by finding the right girl-friend. Richard is considering buying a pet. If you were to ask John what he wanted, he would say a loving wife; Richard would say a faithful pet. Even though John and Richard share the same need for love, their "wants" are different.

ASSIGNMENT 41

Directions:

1. In the Needs Versus Wants Table, list seven needs. You may select them from among those discussed earlier in this unit, or pick some others that you have thought of.

2. Next to each need, fill in one or more things you want to fill those needs.

▼

NEEDS VERSUS WANTS TABLE

NEED	WANT

ASSIGNMENT 42

Directions:

1. Look over the wants you listed in the previous assignment. On a Wants Versus Needs Table, list a few more things you want that don't appear in that assignment.

2. Next to each of these wants, fill in the need or needs that generate that want.

WANTS VERSUS NEEDS TABLE

WANT	NEED

Needs Change

Needs are always there, but the ones that concern you at any one time will change. For example, if you already feel safe and secure, you won't feel those needs very strongly. They have already been met. Of course, if your safety and security are threatened, you will begin to feel these needs again.

Since the needs you are trying to meet change, so will the things you want to have in order to meet them. People without shelter will probably focus on that need until they find a home. Then they will turn their attention to some other need.

Pick Up That Tool!

Your needs influence your thoughts, feelings, and actions. And since they do, they affect your ability to make decisions, and the decisions you make. By understanding your needs, you can select actions that meet them. That's why the tool of recognizing needs is so important to problem solving. So pick it up, and let's march onward.

CHAPTER SUMMARY

In this chapter, you discovered and picked up two more tools. These tools help you recognize your values and your needs. Added to your previous tool of recognizing emotions, you are now prepared for what lies ahead.

As you near Mt. Problem Solving and begin to climb its lower slopes, you come to a narrow passage. A magic door closes off the passage to those without the proper equipment. Fortunately, the tools you have earned are just what you need to open the door and to continue on to the last leg of your journey. Chapter 8 takes you there.

▼

PROBLEM SOLVING

◄◄ UNIT 1 ►►

AN EXAMPLE OF POOR PROBLEM SOLVING

The Meanest and Biggest Punch

James grew up knowing one thing: the person with the meanest and biggest punch always wins. Winning and power became important to him. His dad taught him this. His first experience with power and winning was in preschool, when he was about four years old. He remembers the other children playing and having fun. He also wanted to have fun, so he tried to join a group of children who were throwing a ball around.

James wanted to be part of the group, but Johnny didn't want him to. James remembers Johnny's mean face when he pushed James away. James remembers overwhelming feelings. He doesn't remember exactly what happened next, but he does remember getting thrown out of preschool for beating Johnny up. When he hit Johnny, James felt better. The strong bad feelings went away. He knew he was more important than Johnny because he could beat him up.

When James got home, his father showed him who had the meanest punch. James was confused, but he figured that his father was teaching him how to get better at punching. Maybe he hadn't done a very good job with Johnny. His father was still the best. He knew that because his father taught him by example, and Dad sure had a hard punch.

Through the years, there were many others like Johnny. James never backed down; he always had to prove that he was the best. For a very long time, James thought that winning and power were "what it was all about." And so, through the years, James continued to solve problems in the same way because he knew no other.

He grew tired of adults telling him that fighting didn't work; it sure seemed to work for him. James stopped feeling bad when he fought. He recalled the energy that fighting gave him, and how this was so much better than those bad feelings. So James continued to make the same choice, one he had learned a long time ago.

When James got older, he would often think that his dad would have been proud of him, because he had the meanest punch. But his dad never came to visit him in his cell.

A Choice That May Not Feel Like a Choice

Angry behavior is a choice, but for some people, it may not feel like one.

Whenever James got angry, he either did nothing or he fought. He had a choice, but one with only two options. Many times, neither option was a good one. We call these "forced choices."

James never explored the other alternatives that were open to him. He knew he had a choice not to fight, but that choice did not feel good because of all those bad feelings. If he made that choice, his dad might get angry at him and try to teach him again by showing him a mean punch. Fighting sometimes worked, but sometimes it didn't. James would never hit a girl, so when Francine called him ugly names, he had no option but to do nothing. Sometimes James fought when he had no chance to win, like the time against the three older boys.

Did James Have the Tools?

Did James have the tools you have found to deal with anger and solve problems?

He had never learned to acknowledge and sort out his feelings. All feelings for James resulted in anger. And that meant feeling bad. James did not recognize his needs, and, therefore, was not able to meet them in any other way.

His values influenced his decision to fight, because power and winning were so important to him. But he rarely thought about values, and he never understood that he had many other values that were violated by his violent behavior.

For James, problem solving was a futile exercise. He didn't have the tools to begin with, and he had no idea what he would do with them if he did have them. So he was left with forced choices. Fortunately, you do have the tools. The rest of this chapter will teach you how to use them to solve problems. But first, let's look at just how bad forced choices can be.

ASSIGNMENT 43

Directions:

1. What do you think it feels like to have to make forced choices? Sometimes you may have to choose between something good and something better; sometimes between something bad and something worse. In this assignment, you are going to describe yourself. For each of the forced choices in the following Forced Choices Frame, check the one that best describes you. Maybe neither of the choices describes you, but you must pick one.

This is a fun exercise for other people to try. See if their answers are similar to yours. You can get more Forced Choices Frames from your counselor.

FORCED CHOICES FRAME

Are you more like:

a. a bird _____ or a snake _____

b. a scientist _____ or an athlete _____

c. a druggie _____ or a preppie _____

d. a leader _____ or a follower _____

e. a power ranger _____ or Superman _____

f. morning _____ or night _____

g. a drug pusher _____ or a killer _____

h. an angel _____ or a saint _____

i. James _____ or Sharon _____

Reproduced from *The Angry Self: A Comprehensive Approach to Anger Management*, © 1999, Zeig, Tucker & Co., Publishers.

COMMENTS ON ASSIGNMENT 43

Forced choices are difficult. As you can see from your assignment, very few of these choices could be considered good ones. Choice (e) illustrates how choosing between two ridiculous options can be frustrating. In some cases, you had to choose between reasonable choices, and in other cases, your choice did not seem to matter much. For people who have not explored alternatives, forced choices may be a way in which they approach life. It's pretty frustrating, don't you think?

◀◀ **UNIT 2** ▶▶

THE PROBLEM-SOLVING MODEL

Anger and Problem Solving

Problem solving can be a good companion to anger. Anger is the alarm and problem solving is a positive way of responding to that alarm. Problem solving avoids the forced choices that were so frustrating in the last unit. Here's how it works.

Introducing the Method

Figure 8 illustrates a method for problem solving. The steps seem very simple at first, but some of them require practice to master.

Figure 8. A problem-solving method.

Step 1. Identify the Problem

The steps in this problem-solving method are easy to understand, but can be difficult to do.

The first step is to identify the problem. How hard could that be? If Sally's boss fired her without reason, the problem would be to get her job back. But let's look at the following example.

Carlos sold cars. He was good at his job and normally earned about $4,000 a month in commissions. However, he had lost a sale that he thought should have been a sure thing. The customer had liked the car and was willing to pay the price. But when the customer wanted to take the car out for a test drive, Carlos' manager wouldn't allow it. He said too many cars were being taken out and not returned. The manager said this customer didn't "look right." So Carlos lost the sale.

Why had the manager refused to let the customer take the car for a test drive? Carlos suspected that it was because the customer was Hispanic, but he wasn't sure. Carlos was also Hispanic. He *was* sure of one thing—he was angry.

▼

ASSIGNMENT 44

Directions:

1. Identify Carlos' problem. Write your answer in your notebook.

COMMENTS ON ASSIGNMENT 44

On the surface, you might say that the problem is that Carlos lost the sale and, therefore, his commission. But that is not really the problem; rather, it is the result of the problem.

Going deeper, you might decide that the problem was that the manager had not let Carlos' customer take a car for a test drive. This is indeed a problem because it is very hard to sell a car to someone without the person's trying it out. Yet if the real reason for the manager's refusal was that the customer was likely to steal the car, Carlos could hardly complain.

On the other hand, if the sales manager was prejudiced against Hispanics and would not let one take a car on a test drive, Carlos would have a problem that would come up again and again, costing him a lot of money. That would surely be a problem, but Carlos was not sure that the sales manager was acting out of prejudice.

You would not be wrong if you identified any of the above as a problem in this case. However, the root problem is that Carlos doesn't know whether or not the sales manager acted from prejudice. If he can solve this problem, Carlos can then decide whether any further action is necessary to avoid losing sales in the future.

How to Identify Problems

In most cases, identifying the problem really is very easy. The most important thing is not to jump too quickly to a conclusion. Give yourself a minute or two, if possible, to think about the entire situation. Identify your feelings. Which feelings are uncomfortable? What event or situation contributed to those feelings? The answer to that question is likely to be the problem you should try to solve first.

Consider Carlos' situation. Several feelings were making him uncomfortable, but the main feeling was outrage. Carlos was outraged because he thought that the sales manager might be prejudiced against people like himself. Carlos also felt frustrated because he couldn't do anything about the outrage since he wasn't sure that the manager was indeed prejudiced. What caused the uncomfortable feelings? I think it was Carlos' uncertainty about why his manager had acted as he had.

Once we identify the problem as the uncertainty of the situation, we can readily go on to finding alternatives that will remove this uncertainty.

If you go through the entire problem-solving process and find that none of your solutions seem to "work" the way you want them to work, it is possible that you are trying to solve the wrong problem.

In this case, you should go over the situation carefully in your mind and try to uncover a problem lurking beneath the surface—a problem that must be solved before you can hope to solve the more obvious problems on the surface of the situation. In the foregoing example, if you had identified the problem as Carlos' losing his commission, the alternatives would have led you to a different solution, a solution that did not address Carlos' uncertainty about his supervisor's view of Hispanics.

◄◄ UNIT 3 ►►
FINDING ALTERNATIVES

Step 2. Look for a Solution

The second step in the problem-solving process is to find alternatives that will take care of the problem you identified in the first step.

Carlos' Choices

Before going any further, think about Carlos' problem. Carlos wants to find out if the sales manager acted with prejudice. What alternatives can you think of for Carlos?

ASSIGNMENT 45

Directions:

1. Write down alternatives for Carlos. Don't worry about whether they are good alternatives or even reasonable alternatives—just list all of the alternatives you can think of in your notebook. Spend only 5 or 10 minutes, at most, on this assignment.

The number of alternatives for Carlos that you listed may be small. If it is, don't worry about it. This chapter will help you realize just how many choices you have in most situations. In fact, your list of alternatives may grow so large that you will have to learn another skill—how to quickly weed out the ones that are least promising! Also, your life experiences often form the basis for your alternatives, and these will, of course, increase as you live your life.

Here are just a few of Carlos' alternatives.
- Come right out and ask the sales manager if he is prejudiced.
- Ask the sales manager exactly why he refused the test drive.
- Ask other salespeople if they have observed any prejudicial actions by the sales manager.
- Threaten to beat up the sales manager.
- Beat up the sales manager.
- Shoot the sales manager.
- Shoot the sales manager and all of his family (do you see how ridiculous these alternatives can get?).

▸ Do nothing.

▸ Quit the job.

▸ Tell the whole story to the sales manager's boss—the general manager.

In Unit 4, we will begin evaluating the alternatives (which is step 3), but for now the important idea is that most situations allow a large number of alternative solutions, if you can just think of them.

Hints for Thinking of Alternatives

1. *Take your time.* In most situations, you can spend a few minutes reviewing the situation and coming up with alternatives.

2. *Keep the problem in mind.* In step 1, you identified your problem. As you try to come up with alternatives, don't forget what the problem is. A trick you can use is saying a sentence to yourself and then filling in the blank. Using Carlos as an example: "The problem is to find out if the sales manager is prejudiced, so I will _____."

3. *Keep an open mind.* Don't fall in love with your first idea. As you think of alternatives, you may come across one that seems very good, at least on the surface. At this point, you might shut off other approaches to the problem and focus on variations of that one alternative. For example, if Carlos liked the first alternative he thought of—asking the sales manager if he were prejudiced —he might spend the rest of his time thinking about exactly how he would word the question. Carlos would then miss out on all of the other possible alternatives, some of which might end up being better than the first one.

4. *Be creative.* We tend to think of choices that are similar to ones we have made in the past. This makes sense, because our own life experiences are our best source of alternatives. But there has to be a first time for everything, so try to think of choices that are new to you. Try saying to yourself something like: "Let me see if there is something completely different that might work."

5. *Pretend you are someone else.* Pick someone, real or fictional, whom you feel would handle your current problem well, and then ask yourself, "What would so-and-so do in this situation?" You might come up with a great alternative for yourself.

Practice Makes Perfect

The following assignment will let you practice the skill of finding alternatives.

In this assignment, you are presented with five situations. You should do at least two or three of these. If you feel they are useful, take the time to do all five, even if it means not finishing this unit today.

If you have someone working with you or a friend or two who might be interested, have them work each situation separately from you, and then compare results.

Use Alternatives Frames like the one that follows the assignment to record your result. Your counselor can provide you with more frames.

▼

ASSIGNMENT 46

Directions:

1. For each of the following situations, fill out an Alternatives Frame. There is a time limit on each situation. This time limit applies only to the first item in the Alternatives Frame: listing alternatives. When the time is up, go on to the other items in the frame, but take all the time you need to do these.

Situation A. Jimmy and Sandra are engaged to be married. The wedding is to take place next month. While on her way home from work, Sandra sees Jimmy with his arm around a woman she doesn't recognize. While she watches, it looks as though Jimmy is starting to kiss the other woman, but a bus passes between them and she doesn't see what happens next. When the traffic clears, they are gone. What are Sandra's alternatives? (Time limit: 5 minutes)

Situation B. Mark, a good friend and coworker, missed work yesterday and the day before. When you called him after work yesterday evening, he said that aliens from the planet Schnorb were visiting him and he had to stay home and answer their questions. You thought he must have been drunk or joking, but Mark didn't come to work today either. So you go to his apartment at lunch. Mark lets you in. He is alone, but when you came in, he was talking to someone who doesn't appear to be there. What are your choices? (Time limit: 7 minutes)

Situation C. Brent, whom you know only slightly, is selling his car. The price seems to be low, you need a car, and so you talk to Brent. He lets you drive around for a while. You like the car and decide that you want to buy it, but you want to have your mechanic check it over first. Brent says he's sorry, but he's selling the car because he has to move to another town and is leaving in one hour. If he doesn't sell the car by then, a dealer will buy it for $200 less. So you buy the car. Two days later, it breaks down in traffic and your mechanic tells you that it will cost $1,500 to fix it. What are your alternatives? (Time limit: 7 minutes)

Situation D. It may seem like a small thing, but at least twice a week you go outside to find that people have let their dogs make messes in your front yard. You have to clean them up. In your city, people are supposed to clean up after their dogs, but the fine for not doing so is only $10. What can you do about this situation? (Time limit: 5 minutes)

Situation E. Mr. Clemens, your science teacher, gives really hard multiple-choice tests. A few kids in the class always seem to know the answers, but you struggle to get mediocre grades. Almost half of the class cheats by copying from the papers of the "A" students whenever they can. You don't do this because you think it's wrong, and you only want the grade you really earn. Halfway through the course, Mr. Clemens announces that the final grades will be curved: the top four students will get As, the next six students will get Bs, the next six students Cs, and the bottom four will get Ds. You probably would have been given a B except for the seven or eight cheaters, who now will move ahead of you on the curve, knocking your grade down to a C, or even a D. What are your alternatives? (Time limit: 10 minutes)

▼

ALTERNATIVES FRAME

WHAT IS THE SITUATION?	
ITEM	**YOUR ANSWER**
List alternatives (leave out ones that are totally absurd). Number each alternative.	
Which alternatives don't even address the problem? (List their numbers here and scratch them out above.)	
What caused you to stop listing alternatives? (Check one.)	___ I ran out of time. ___ I ran out of ideas. ___ I got stuck listing variations of one idea. ___ Other (specify:_____)
Be creative: list one or two other choices (if you can) that are very different from the ones you already have listed.	
Pretend you are somebody else. What would that person do?	Person: What he or she would do: Person: What he or she would do:

EVALUATING ALTERNATIVES

Step 3. Describe Which Choice Is Best

Now that you have generated a list of alternatives, you are faced with the task of choosing one. Naturally, you want to choose the "best" one, but what does "best" mean? Most important, a good alternative is one that solves the problem. But there are other considerations that go into finding the best choice, such as:

- ▶ Is the alternative something that you are able to do?
- ▶ Does the alternative coincide with your values and needs?
- ▶ What are the costs of the alternative?
- ▶ What are the benefits of the alternative?

"You Pass, You Fail"

One way to evaluate alternatives is to assign each one a grade—A is the best grade and F is the worst. To assign the grade, you can examine the good points, or "pros," and bad points, "cons," of the alternative.

As an example, let's examine a few of Carlos' alternatives.

Alternative 1: "Come right out and ask the sales manager if he is prejudiced." First, does this alternative solve the problem? The answer is, "Maybe." If the sales manager would definitely tell the truth, the problem would be solved—Carlos would know for sure whether the sales manager was prejudiced and could then take further action, if necessary. But the sales manager might not tell the truth, so this alternative might not solve the problem. Now let's look at our other criteria.

"Is the alternative something Carlos can do?" Yes.

"Does the alternative coincide with Carlos' needs and values?" Probably it does. This approach is honest and straightforward; there is not much to object to here.

"What are the costs?" There could be a great cost. The sales manager might be offended by the question and take actions, such as recommending that Carlos be fired.

"What are the benefits?" Other than possibly solving the problem, this alternative has no obvious benefits.

What kind of a grade does this alternative get? I would probably give it a C- because it may not solve the problem and there are great potential costs.

Alternative 3: "Ask other salespeople if they had observed any prejudicial actions by the sales manager." This one is more likely than Alternative 1 to solve the problem, unless, of course, the sales manager has been very good at hiding his feelings. Carlos might have a bit of a values problem with it, however, since it smacks of "sneakiness." The costs are probably minimal, unless a colleague decides to tell the sales manager about Carlos' question. A potential benefit is that, if there really is a problem, Carlos will have taken the first steps toward getting support from his coworkers. The final grade—perhaps a B-.

Alternative 6: "Shoot the sales manager." This one gets an F without really having to evaluate it too much. Some alternatives can be thrown out almost as soon as you think of them.

Going Out to Dinner

Let's leave Carlos now and go on to another situation where you will be presented with several opportunities to list and evaluate alternatives.

You have been invited out to dinner by your girlfriend's parents. Your girlfriend, Charlene, is there, and so are her parents, her brother, and her brother's girlfriend. This is the first time you have been out with Charlene's parents. You want them to like you, so you want to create a good impression. Because this is important to you, you are feeling some anxiety. You keep thinking, "I hope I don't goof up."

The parents take you to a very nice restaurant. You look around and note that everyone is appropriately dressed. You're glad you decided to wear your good suit. The hostess greets everyone at the entrance and escorts you all to the table. You are not sure where everyone is supposed to sit.

ASSIGNMENT 47

Directions:

1. Use the following Alternatives Evaluation Frame to list five reasonable alternatives for solving the problem, "How do I decide where to sit?" For each one, evaluate the pros and cons and then give a final grade. If you need additional forms, you can get them from your counselor.

▼

ALTERNATIVES EVALUATION FRAME

PROBLEM: How do I decide where to sit?

ALTERNATIVE 1
   Pros:
   Cons:
   Grade:

ALTERNATIVE 2
   Pros:
   Cons:
   Grade:

ALTERNATIVE 3
   Pros:
   Cons:
   Grade:

ALTERNATIVE 4
   Pros:
   Cons:
   Grade:

ALTERNATIVE 5
   Pros:
   Cons:
   Grade:

One good alternative would be to wait until Charlene's parents sit down, and then to pick out adjoining seats and pull out one of the chairs for your girlfriend. (Don't forget to take the seat next to her!) This may not be your favorite alternative; that's perfectly okay. Each person brings his or her own set of feelings, values, and needs to every situation, so that what is good for one person may not be nearly as good for another.

An Easy Choice

Let's go on with the evening. Everyone at the table seems to be in a good mood, so you start to relax. You tell yourself that everything is going just fine. (That's positive self-talk, and it always helps.)

The waiter asks everyone what they would like to drink. You are not of legal drinking age, but you would like a beer. Unfortunately, Charlene knows you are too young, and she has ordered iced tea. Besides, the embarrassment of being "carded" is too great a risk to take at this time. So, this is an easy situation because you can reject the alternative of trying to get a beer without too much thought.

The Dreaded "Menu"

After the waiter brings the drinks, he gives out menus. Since a menu is nothing more than a list of choices, it's pretty clear that you have a problem to solve: what should you order? Normally, this would not be a difficult situation, but the fates are against you this evening.

When you open the menu, you see a very long list of choices, a lot of which look good. There are also some that you really don't care for (such as the calf's brains), and a few others you don't even understand (what is a "John Dory" anyway?).

Just then, Charlene's mother asks you a question. You become involved in the conversation, so you pay little attention to the menu. Wouldn't you know, this is the evening when the waiter is in a hurry, so he comes back to take orders in just a few minutes. You see him approaching your table, a determined look in his eye that clearly says, "I'm ready to take your order." His notepad is out, and his pencil is positioned for writing. "Are you all ready to order?" he asks. You clearly are not, but you hesitate to say anything. "What if everyone else wants to order now?" you ask yourself.

ASSIGNMENT 48

Directions:

1. Use the following Alternatives Evaluation Frame to list five reasonable alternative solutions to the current problem. If you need additional frames, get them from your counselor.

▼

ALTERNATIVES EVALUATION FRAME

PROBLEM:

Do I say anyting to the waiter or do I just order? If so, what do I order?

ALTERNATIVE 1

  Pros:

  Cons:

  Grade:

ALTERNATIVE 2

  Pros:

  Cons:

  Grade:

ALTERNATIVE 3

  Pros:

  Cons:

  Grade:

ALTERNATIVE 4

  Pros:

  Cons:

  Grade:

ALTERNATIVE 5

  Pros:

  Cons:

  Grade:

COMMENTS ON ASSIGNMENT 48

You may have already got the hang of evaluating alternatives. In that case, you really don't have to read the rest of these comments. If you are not sure that you are on the right track, take a look at how I might have handled Assignment 48.

  Alternative 1: Pick anything out of the menu, and just order it. Hopefully, if you happen to pick John Dory, it won't turn out to be a porcupine. (Actually, it's a fish.)

  Pros and cons: If you pick something from the menu without really looking at your choices, you may end up with a meal you won't like. Nothing really terrible will happen (unless you accidentally pick something to which you are allergic). You might not enjoy your meal, but no one will probably notice, unless you are so turned off by the food that you don't eat it. Your girlfriend's parents might think that is rude. Of course, you might well be giving up the opportunity for something really tasty, and so would be cheating yourself.

Grade: This choice would probably get a grade of C. It's an average choice—not the best, not the worst.

Alternative 2: Don't order anything.

Pros and cons: If you decide not to order anything, you will go hungry. You worry that your stomach will make funny noises, and everyone will think that you are a noisy dork. You are convinced that you will look silly. The other people at the table will ask you what's wrong, and their concern will further embarrass you.

Grade: This is not a good alternative. Just thinking about it created uncomfortable feelings! This alternative rates a grade of D-.

Alternative 3: Tell the waiter you need a little more time.

Pros and cons: This will give you an opportunity to look at the menu, although the others will have to wait for you. When you considor this choice, you start worrying that your girlfriend and her family will think that you can't make decisions. But everyone is having such a good time, they probably will not mind your taking more time to decide.

Grade: You may feel a little embarrassed, but this looks like a good choice and gets a grade of B+.

You Have to Make a Choice Sometime

Okay, no more stalling. Let's pick out a main course. There are at least 50 choices. Your list of alternatives is too large, so you have to quickly get rid of some. Since you are not in the mood for fish, you eliminate those choices. You also decide to skip anything that you don't understand, since there are plenty of good choices you do know about.

Well, that brings it down to 35 choices. You decide that chicken or steak sounds the best, so you throw out all of the vegetarian, lamb, and veal entrees. That leaves 10 different chicken and five different steak dinners.

As you look at the menu, you are aware of the waiter, who is patiently standing in the corner waiting for you to put your menu down. That's how he will know that you are ready to order. Your girlfriend's dad seems to have put his menu down already. It's time to decide.

You focus on two chicken dishes, both of which sound healthy and delicious: chicken with shallots and wild mushrooms, and chicken and dumplings. Chicken and dumplings is one of your favorite meals, but you are feeling adventurous tonight and so decide on the other entree.

You put your menu down, and the waiter immediately picks up on your cue. He comes over to your table, and everyone starts ordering. When it is your turn to order, you are ready. You tell the waiter what you would like, and he looks up from his notepad with an apologetic expression: "Sorry, Sir, we are out of wild mushrooms."

ASSIGNMENT 49

Directions:

1. Use the following Alternatives Evaluation Frame to list five reasonable alternatives to the current problem. If you need additional frames, get them from your counselor.

ALTERNATIVES EVALUATION FRAME

PROBLEM: What do I order now? Or should I ask for still more time? Or . . .

ALTERNATIVE 1
  Pros:
  Cons:
  Grade:

ALTERNATIVE 2
  Pros:
  Cons:
  Grade:

ALTERNATIVE 3
  Pros:
  Cons:
  Grade:

ALTERNATIVE 4
  Pros:
  Cons:
  Grade:

ALTERNATIVE 5
  Pros:
  Cons:
  Grade:

Actually, this is not much of a problem. Your problem-solving process resulted in your listing a large number of alternatives. From these, you narrowed the field of choices to just two, and then picked one of those two. Since your first choice was not available, you just fall back on the next best alternative. Chicken and dumplings sounds just fine.

You feel really good about yourself; you handled that situation very well. Pat yourself on the back (but not when the others are looking—they might not understand).

◀◀ UNIT 5 ▶▶
CHOOSING AN ALTERNATIVE

There isn't too much to say about choosing an alternative. Once you have listed alternatives and evaluated them, the choice is easy—just pick the alternative with the highest grade.

Putting Your Choice to the Test

The next to last thing you need to do is to ask yourself if your choice solves the problem. It is very easy to become so absorbed in the process of listing and evaluating alternatives that you lose track of the problem you are trying to solve. Then, when you pick an alternative and act on it, you end up finding out that you didn't solve the problem at all.

If this happens, all you need to do is discard the faulty choice and choose the alternative with the next highest grade. If all of your acceptable alternatives fail to solve the problem, there are two common causes: you haven't identified the problem properly, or the problem has no acceptable solution.

Problems Without Solutions

Are there problems that simply don't have any acceptable solutions? I think there are, but they are not very common. In most cases, a problem that appears to lack solutions has not been properly recognized. For example, suppose the woman you love marries someone else. You are very sad, frustrated, depressed, and, in general, feeling "bad." If you state the problem as, "How can I get her back?" your alternatives will probably all be unacceptable, such as:

▸ Kill her husband.

▸ Kidnap her and make her see she really loves you.

▸ Ruin their life together so they will divorce.

You may be able to think of a few more, but I doubt if you can come up with an alternative that is acceptable to you and will really work.

Is this a problem without a solution? I don't think it is. The real problem is that you have "bad" feelings that are making you uncomfortable and unhappy. So the problem is, "How can I get rid of my feelings of sadness, frustration, and depression?" Now you have a huge number of alternatives, some of which are bound to be acceptable to you. Some examples are:

▸ Begin socializing again and find another girlfriend.

- Take a trip (I'm referring to travel, not pot).
- Start a new hobby.
- Keep busy with your work.
- Print 100 photos of your ex-girlfriend and bury them.

Some of these alternatives clearly are better than others, but my point is that you have a lot of good choices when you state the problem properly.

Let's go back to the original question: Are there problems without solutions? While most such problems can be solved by stating them differently, some problems truly have no solution that you can implement. If you fear we all will be destroyed in a nuclear war, your problem could be stated: "How can I get rid of my fear of being killed in a nuclear war?" You might find that your best alternative is simply to understand that there is nothing you can do to remove your fear, and, therefore, you will have to learn to live with it. This is, in itself, actually a solution to your problem; it just isn't a very complete one.

You might think that problem solving failed in this case. I'll admit that it didn't help you come up with an ideal solution, but it did two good things. First, you found the best solution available. Second, because you now know that you did all you could do, you can stop worrying about what to do. That alone can be quite a relief.

James' Next to Last Problem

Don't worry—James is not about to die. He is still alive, well, and making real progress in his life, as you will read in the last chapter. This is simply James' next to last problem in this workbook. At this time, James was still working with his counselor. They were just starting on problem solving. You will quickly see that James has not yet acquired the skills you have learned. Therefore, we are going to stop this story in places and try to put James back on the right track.

Here is the situation. James is back in high school. The school dance is next Saturday night. His girlfriend, Amy, expects him to take her to the dance. His boss expects him to work. He thinks to himself: "How am I going to take Amy to the dance and still go to work?"

ASSIGNMENT 50

Directions:

1. James has just stated his problem. Clearly. it has no solution. Restate his problem. Write your answer in your notebook.

COMMENTS ON ASSIGNMENT 50

There are really a number of ways to state James' problem so that we can find alternatives. One way is, "Should I take Amy to the dance or go to work?" Let's use this one because it has two clear alternatives.

James Waffles

Let's back up. James asks himself, "Should I take Amy to the dance or go to work?" He sits on the sofa in the living room and ponders the problem. "If I hadn't missed two days last week when I was sick, I could ask my boss for a day off, but he would never go for it now. If I don't take Amy to the dance, she'll probably go with Bill, and who knows if I'll ever get her back. If Amy stops loving me, who will? My boss will definitely not give me time off, and if I don't show up, he'll fire me. I should have told Amy last week—maybe she wouldn't be so angry with me. This is a good job and I don't want to lose it. Besides, I promised my boss I would stick with it."

I'll stop James' thoughts here. They went on like this for 10 minutes. At the end of that time, he still had not made a decision. He had, however, become very anxious. What went wrong? If James had your problem-solving skills, he would have realized that he had two alternatives. Take a moment to think of what they are before you read the next paragraph.

James' two alternatives are:
► Take Amy to the dance.
► Go to work.

Actually, there is at least one more alternative—don't take Amy to the dance and don't go to work—but that one is so poor that even James rejected it without giving it further thought.

James was evaluating these alternatives, but he was doing so in such a disorganized fashion that he never could give each one a "grade." You, however, should have no such difficulty.

ASSIGNMENT 51

Directions:

1. One of the alternatives is for James to go to work. What feelings does he talk about that cause him to dislike this alternative?

2. What value causes James to dislike the alternative of skipping work and taking Amy to the dance?

3. If James does not take Amy to the dance, he fears that one of his basic needs will not be met. Which need?

Read the first part of the "Comments on Assignment 51" that follow the Alternatives Evaluation Frame. Then come back and do part 4 of this assignment.

4. Use the following Alternatives Evaluation Frame to evaluate the two alternatives.

▼

ALTERNATIVES EVALUATION FRAME

PROBLEM:

Should I take Amy to the dance or should I go to work?

ALTERNATIVE 1

Take Amy to the dance and miss work.

   Pros:

   Cons:

   Grade:

ALTERNATIVE 2

Go to work and skip the dance.

   Pros:

   Cons:

   Grade:

COMMENTS ON ASSIGNMENT 51

The answers to the first three parts are:

1. Jealousy—James doesn't like the idea of Bill's going to the dance with Amy.

2. Honor—James promised his boss he would stick to the job, and he doesn't want to go back on that promise. This value could also be considered "honesty."

3. The need to be loved—James feels that Amy loves him and he needs that love. The fact that James has other love, such as his mother's, doesn't mean that he won't also feel a need for Amy's love.

You may have come up with other answers that are equally valid. The important thing to get out of this exercise is that your tools of recognizing feelings, values, and needs can help define the major pros and cons of each alternative.

Return to the assignment and do part 4 before reading further.

Both of these alternatives have pros and cons, so some people will choose going to work and some will choose going to the dance. Which alternative you graded higher depends a lot on your own values, needs, and feelings. For the purposes of this unit, choose one.

▼

James Makes a Choice

Once more, we go back and rescue James. He had gone through the process of evaluating the two alternatives and decided to go to work. (No hissing and booing from those of you who picked differently.) Now all he has left is to do it. Going to work is the easy part; the hard part is telling Amy. As is often the case, solving one problem has led to another: "How should I tell Amy I can't go to the dance?"

James' Last Problem

Well, James, we have the whole problem-solving process to help you decide.

ASSIGNMENT 52

Directions:

1. Use the Alternatives Evaluation Frame to solve James' last problem. Don't just come up with alternative ways of saying, "I can't take you because I have to work." See if you can think of things James can do to make it more likely that he can keep Amy as a girlfriend, and perhaps even improve their relationship. I'll start you off by giving you Alternative 1.

▼

ALTERNATIVES EVALUATION FRAME

PROBLEM:

How should I tell Amy I can't take her to the dance?

ALTERNATIVE 1

Let Amy know how much you care about her. Explain why you cannot go to the dance and apologize for not telling her sooner.

  Pros:

  Cons:

  Grade:

ALTERNATIVE 2

  Pros:

  Cons:

  Grade:

ALTERNATIVE 3

  Pros:

  Cons:

  Grade:

ALTERNATIVE 4

  Pros:

  Cons:

  Grade:

ALTERNATIVE 5

  Pros:

  Cons:

  Grade:

◀◀ UNIT 6 ▶▶
PROBLEMS ARE PUZZLES

Why is it so difficult to solve the real problems we all encounter in our lives? The problem-solving skills presented in this chapter are really not that hard to learn. The assignments were almost *too* simple. Why, then, is it so difficult to apply these techniques to real-life problems?

Problem = Obstacle

Actually, it is *not* hard to apply problem solving. But some people have mental "blocks" that stop them from getting started. Although it happens to almost all of us at one time or another, for some it happens constantly. To understand this "block," think of the word "problem." What comes to mind? One common association is "obstacle." A "problem" is something that gets in our way and is hard to get around—something that "blocks" us.

Puzzle = Challenge

Now think about another word—"puzzle." What images does "puzzle" bring to mind? To me, a puzzle is a challenge. We "solve" puzzles and we "meet" challenges. A puzzle is not an obstacle; it doesn't block us. A puzzle motivates us to find a solution.

Unclimbable Mountains Versus Challenging Hills

Figure 9 is a graphical representation of problems and puzzles.

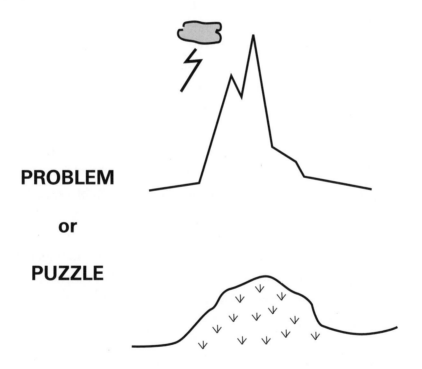

PROBLEM

or

PUZZLE

Figure 9. A "problem" is like a mountain and a "puzzle" is like a hill.

In Figure 9, the word "problem" has triggered a mental image of an unclimbable mountain. We reach the base of the mountain and become discouraged and frustrated. Perhaps we pick up loose stones that have rolled down the slopes and fling them back at the mountain. It doesn't do any good. The mountain doesn't care, and the stones just bounce back downhill and and we have to dodge them.

On the other hand, the word "puzzle" brings to mind a hill. It may be a bit of a challenge to get to the top, but we never doubt for a moment that we can do it. It's actually fun to do the climb, and reaching the top makes us feel happy and confident.

It's Your Call

When a situation occurs in your life that requires a solution, you can think of it as a problem or you can think of it as a puzzle. You have that choice. The way that you choose to think of the situation will determine whether it is easy to solve or very difficult.

My advice is to think positively. When a situation presents itself, say to yourself: "I can solve this puzzle. I have the skills. I know how to solve problems by thinking of them as puzzles. And I know that when I have solved the puzzle, it will feel great."

Emotions Can Get in the Way

It would be easy to think of problems as puzzles if we did not have strong feelings and thoughts associated with these situations. These emotions can get in the way of our ability to think positively; they can make that challenging hill look exactly like an unclimbable mountain.

Consider Sharon and her friend Trisha. Sharon is good at math. She actually enjoys the homework in her statistics class. When Sharon took the final exam, she looked at each question as a puzzle. She calmly went about reading the questions, making sure she understood them, and applying her knowledge to solving the puzzles. Since she knew enough about statistics to answer most of them, she got a good grade.

Trisha actually knows as much about statistics as Sharon. But Trisha has hated math since the third grade. When she looked at a question on the final exam, Trisha saw a "problem." She became anxious, and the problem became a mountain. She tried to climb the mountain, but gave up in despair. Trisha never got to apply her knowledge, and she ended up with a poor grade in the class.

The difference between Sharon's "A" and Trisha's "D" was almost entirely attitude. Sharon just "knew" she could solve the puzzles, and Trisha "knew" she could never overcome the problems.

What does this mean to you? You are now like Sharon. You can deal effectively with life's situations by using your problem-solving skills. I always knew you could. Now you know it, too.

▼

CONCLUSION

And so we come to the end of our journey. You have learned to deal with anger in a positive and powerful way. Skills that were at first strange and difficult to master have become familiar friends. You have also learned to solve problems. This may be the most important skill you possess. With it, the impossible becomes not only possible, but often *easy*.

Think about who you thought you were when you began this workbook and compare it with who you are now.

ASSIGNMENT 53

Directions:

1. For each of the following traits, rate yourself both as you were when you started this workbook and as you are now. Use a scale of 1 to 10, with 10 being the greatest presence of the trait. Each person changes in different ways. How did this workbook change you?

a. In control	Before _____	Now _____
b. Self-confident	Before _____	Now _____
c. Strong	Before _____	Now _____
d. A good decision maker	Before _____	Now _____
e. Happy	Before _____	Now _____
f. Understanding of others' faults	Before _____	Now _____
g. Able to get what I need	Before _____	Now _____
h. Sharing	Before _____	Now _____
i. Aware of other people's feelings	Before _____	Now _____

Sharon: The End of Her Story

As you have seen, Sharon left her abusive relationship and struggled through a difficult divorce. Her counselor was a big help, but most of the effort was Sharon's, and most of the applause is for her. Sharon completed her graduate studies in counseling, and is currently working in her field, primarily with abused women. She is happy with her work and is quite successful.

Sharon has experienced no further episodes of aggressive anger, but she doesn't "stuff" her anger either. "After such a revelation," she said one day, "how could I?" Sharon has become assertive, and lets people know what she wants in a manner that shows her respect for herself and others. In fact, at one point, her friends had to tell her that she was overdoing it just a bit. Sharon was becoming aggressive. But her respect for others made her realize that she was happiest getting what she wanted without trampling on other people.

Romantically, Sharon had a rough time. After her abusive first marriage, she had grave doubts about relationships. She first had to learn to trust herself and her judgment, and that took time. She didn't date seriously again for over a year. Finally, Sharon began to realize that listening to her feelings would guide her to relationships that would be rewarding to her. As her ability to trust herself and others grew, her ability to love returned. After three and a half years, Sharon met Barry.

Within a year, they married, and things are going very well. If you don't believe me, just ask Melinda. Well, actually Melinda is only seven months old and doesn't talk much, but if she could, she would tell you that Mommy and Daddy are the greatest.

James: The End of His Story

James' journey was more painful. He remained on parole until his 18th birthday. He had learned well, but his problem with anger was deep and hard to eliminate completely. There were several times when the old James showed through, and once he nearly went to jail again. This time, it would have been an adult prison. His former parole officer intervened to convince a judge to give James one more chance. As a young adult, he was sentenced to two years of probation and 100 hours of community service.

Since James had few job skills, for his community service he ended up as a janitor in the county hospital. He had no idea at the time, but this was to be a turning point in his life.

He did such a conscientious job at the hospital that, when his community service was over, they offered him a janitorial job on the night shift. The job paid enough for James to live on, and he was even able to save a few dollars. He was used to living simply, and had few material wants.

James stayed with his therapy after his release, and continued to make progress. When he finally discovered that his anger was deeply rooted in years of physical and emotional abuse, he was able to get in touch with the sadness and the hurt. At times, he struggled to keep his anger, in an effort to avoid the sadness and disappointment he felt because of his lost innocence and childhood. But James also knew how dangerous his anger could be, and how it never got him what he wanted.

James is now 23 years old. He has a girlfriend (he always has a girlfriend, but this one seems to be special) who has never seen his angry face, and, according to James, never will. He worked at the hospital for two years, being promoted to assistant manager of the custodial staff. With the money he was able to save, he opened his own janitorial service. Now he has several young people working for him. He says that they remind him of a younger James. He likes to help young people get started. However, he sets clear limits in his business, and is a very demanding boss. He is also a very caring one.

Get ready for a real surprise—James also attends college, and this is what he enjoys doing most. He has taken many courses in philosophy, pointing out that this is his last chance to find some meaning in the nightmare that he lived. He still lives with ghosts, although he continues to work hard to keep them permanently buried. But James will be all right. It was a long and difficult journey for him, with every discovery a painful experience. Sometimes the memories catch him off guard. That is when he really works hard at making his body relax, and stopping the memories. He said as the memories no longer serve any purpose, there is no point in entertaining them. So he stops them whenever they creep up. He is making good choices, and is feeling empowered.

You: The Beginning of Your Story

James made a remarkable recovery from a nearly disastrous beginning. He had nothing to begin with that you don't also have. You, too, can make good choices. You have the tools, and now you must care enough to use them to empower you for the rest of your life.

Anger is a choice. Choose well. Be successful.